The Team Discovered

Dialogic Team Coaching

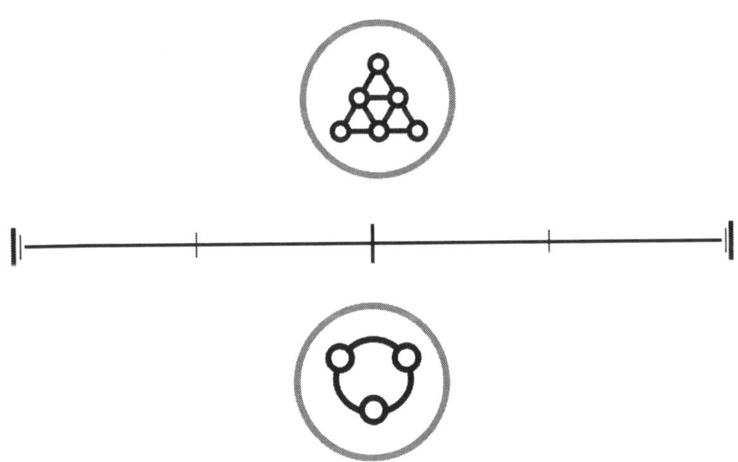

BENNETT H. BRATT

BMI Publishing
Bushe-Marshak Institute for Dialogic Organization Development
3898 Trenton Place
North Vancouver, BC
Canada V7R 3G5
www.b-m-institute.com

Library and Archives Canada Cataloguing in Publication
Title: The team discovered: dialogic team coaching / Bennett H. Bratt.
Names: Bratt, Bennett H., 1963- author.
Description: Series statement: BMI series in dialogic organization development | Includes bibliographical references.
Identifiers: Canadiana 20200228161 | ISBN 9781777184605 (softcover)
Subjects: LCSH: Teams in the workplace—Management. | LCSH: Employees—Coaching of. | LCSH: Leadership.
Classification: LCC HD66 .B73 2020 | DDC 658.4/092—dc23

ISBN: 9781777184605
Imprint: BMI Publishing

Cover and interior design: Vancouver Desktop Publishing Centre

Contents

Foreword by the Series Editors / 5

Acknowledgments / 6

INTRODUCTION

Our scope, purpose, and challenge / 7

PART ONE
Context and Concepts / 11

ONE

Diving In: Musing on a Fish Tank / 12

TWO

The Underpinnings of a Mindset / 17

THREE

Defining Terms and Comparing Mindsets / 29

FOUR

A Case for the Dialogic Path Forward / 36

PART TWO
Entry and Contracting / 45

FIVE

Two Mapmakers / 46

SIX

Approaching the Gatekeeper / 50

PART THREE
Discovery / 53

SEVEN

Leaving the Familiar Behind / 54

EIGHT

Priming the Pump / 58

NINE

Feeling the Fog but Seeing the Light / 63

PART FOUR

Mining, Focusing, and Owning / 69

TEN

Plan/No Plan / 70

ELEVEN

Deciphering and Making Meaning / 72

TWELVE

A Quiet Statement of Focus and Ownership / 75

PART FIVE

Pragmatic Improvements / 79

THIRTEEN

The Salient Sea / 80

FOURTEEN

Clarity / 83

PART SIX

Exit / 89

FIFTEEN

The Meaning Made / 90

SIXTEEN

A Wholesome Meal / 64

Conclusion and Implications / 97

Foreword by the Series Editors

The term *Dialogic Organization Development* was first used in a 2009 article we published in *The Journal of Applied Behavioral Science*. In that article, we wanted to describe how we had seen organization development evolve and contrast it with the original form of OD, which we labeled Diagnostic OD. We were unhappy with how OD textbooks continued to treat the newer premises and practices as if they fit the earlier model. We wanted to create a space for people to think about, research, develop, and discuss these newer approaches to change. This book series is a continuation of that ambition and purpose.

Dialogic OD is a still developing mindset (rather than a set of specific methods). It is rooted in two key intellectual movements that are influencing all social science: how social reality is constructed, maintained, and changed by how we talk (postmodernism), and how social systems emerge and self-organize without leadership direction or a plan (complexity). We have written several articles and book chapters about this, and readers of this book (and all books in the series) are encouraged to access our website, https://b-m-institute.com. Most of our writings and those of some others are available there for free. The articles and book chapters at the website provide a general overview of the theory of Dialogic OD, how it is the same and different from Diagnostic OD, and the basic ideas about leadership, consulting, change, and creating great organizations embedded in Dialogic OD.

Since 2005 we have devoted much of our time and attention to conceptualizing and explaining Dialogic OD. Now we are turning our attention to encouraging presentations of specific dialogic practices applicable to all change methods and approaches. Each of the books in this series is a short, focused, and most important, practical exploration of one topic intended to continue expanding the theory and practice of Dialogic OD. We hope you enjoy the books. We welcome proposals for further volumes.

If you are relatively new to this set of ideas, you can download and read the free "Companion Pre-Reading for Books in the Dialogic OD Series" by requesting it from https://b-m-institute.com.

Gervase R. Bushe
Robert J. Marshak
July 2019

Acknowledgments

Heartfelt thanks to the teams I love. First and foremost, Brenda, Ariana, and Jordan Bratt—the home team, for your patience, inspiration, and belief.

Critically, the numerous, courageous client teams, leaders, and HR professionals who daily offer living laboratories for the concepts described in this book. We are travelers on a shared journey of discovery.

More expansively, to the people that have shaped my story: My current collaborators at The Team Effectiveness Project in Bothell, Washington, USA, including Barrett Horne, Bob Polk, David Firth, George Brewster, Greg Flynn, Paul O'Beirne, Serena Gallenstein, Shannon Patterson, and Sherry Johnson-Metz, plus Mark Meadows at Microsoft and Tracey Johnson and Emily Jarvis at Yukon Government; the internal teams at Ford Motor Company, Volkswagen USA, Sun Microsystems, and T-Mobile; the people and communities that patiently fostered my learning journey, including my extended Bratt and Dykstra clans in the US and Canada; my community of origin in Grand Rapids, Michigan; Calvin University, Tulane University, and Michigan State University; plus numerous partners, mentors, and disrupters.

Finally, this book would not exist without close partnership from: this series' editors Gervase Bushe, PhD and Bob Marshak, PhD, especially for their continued optimism that our spheres of wonder overlap in generative ways; insightful and patient readers of various drafts of this manuscript, including Ariana Bratt, Brenda Bratt, Joel Bratt, Leslie Osborn, and Marian Davis; reviewers Geoff Bellman, Peter Block, John Boudreau, Kristy Feldkamp, Joe Garbus, and Mike Murray; and copyeditor Monique Peterson, whose incisive comments, deft touch, and deep professionalism made finishing this project possible.

Bennett Bratt,
Bothell, Washington USA,
April 22, 2020

INTRODUCTION

Our scope, purpose, and challenge

Teams have been a part of our existence for eons. As the fabric of our daily existence is formed and expressed in small social ecosystems, our fates individually and collectively are intertwined in how well these collections of individuals adhere, achieve, conflict, succeed, or fail toward their particular ends.

Deepened understanding of these small social ecosystems has emerged over time in fields such as sociology, psychology, and anthropology. More specifically, the field of Organization Development (OD) has developed theoretical perspectives on teams that influence the ways leaders lead, researchers study, and practitioners support teams. The corpus is deep and wide, and many fine volumes are available.

In recent years, OD practitioners and researchers have sampled from two mindsets, in many ways both valid and providing utility: The Diagnostic and the Dialogic.

From our heritage, we have available existing **Diagnostic** mindsets, which are primarily oriented toward painting objective pictures of reality and a mode of OD work in which expertise is brought to bear to diagnose teams with all available precision, often utilizing exacting measures, normative data, and predictive models.

A second mindset has come to share center stage. This has been described compellingly as the **Dialogic** mindset (Bushe & Marshak, 2009) (see the free "Companion Booklet to the BMI Series in Dialogic OD" at https://b-m-institute.com). In it, insights from complexity science, a postmodern appreciation of the role of narrative in shaping our sense of reality, and resultant use of narrative inquiry and generative imagery for understanding human systems all combine to help teams find new insights and paths for development.

This Dialogic mindset is further shaped and bolstered by broader understandings of our world that arise in systemic and ecological paradigms. These give us a lens to see our world less as driven by mechanistic forces with anticipatable outcomes, but rather more as a constantly unfolding expression of innumerable forces, some known, some not, that emerge within rough probabilities rather than direct causality (see Thomas Homer-Dixon's excellent 2009 article).

In all transparency, while comparison of these two OD mindsets and practices is an explicit and implicit part of this book, you will find me advocating primarily for the power and utility of the Dialogic approach for understanding teams and their effectiveness, although both mindsets bring gifts to the party. It will all boil down to the lenses we use when we look at teams and our core intent in our interactions with them. During these times of experimentation, how might we embrace the core mindsets and tenets of the Dialogic approach, while also adapting for continued use of parts of the Diagnostic toolbox?

I'll also be taking more of an anthropological approach and considering two additional contemporary facets of organizations and the teams that inhabit them: first, the enormous *compositional and contextual diversity* of teams, and second, their members' *attention poverty*. Given these forces, I will argue that when we see teams for what they are using Dialogic lenses, we begin to see each team as unique. By unique, I mean any and every team is radically different from any other. Given each team's incomparable diversity, the complex and compressing forces at work, and the unique narrative each individual and team writes about itself, any team stands as its own unique social ecosystem.

Further, the Diagnostic mindset is significantly rooted in comparison. In this paradigm, teams can be compared to one another, to averaged and abstracted characteristics derived from studies with large sample populations, to idealized teams deemed "great," and to mythical archetypes of teams. But when we swim in those waters, when we go first and foremost to predictive models and normative data that have at their core a comparison, it's all too easy to lose our focus on the figure in the picture, the very subject of our search for understanding: the team we sit in and with.

Looking at teams with curiosity and awe presents a great opportunity to examine our mental models and test them for relevance, utility, and impact. From these models questions arise that we will take up: How do we help team leaders and members assess a team's current state? Who determines what's most needed to improve effectiveness?

Part exploration of paradigm and part illustrative story, this book is shaped by my experience of Dialogic principles and use of Diagnostic tools, the impossibly difficult circumstances teams and their leaders all too often find themselves in, and my years of experience leading organizations and coaching teams.

To manage the scope of this endeavor, almost everything written addresses the practice of supporting teams from the vantage point of a *single team*. I believe this is our most useful starting point. No doubt, there is great value to researching large numbers of teams, but we must keep these two vantage points very separate. We will be very clear that research into large numbers of teams that is subsequently applied back to a single team commits a common but significant logical fallacy (the Ecological fallacy as per King, Rosen, and Tanner, 2004, to be specific). I believe the implications of this are worth testing, as fallacy of any sort should not be our calling card. This will become clear as we go.

I offer a starter set of implications we will explore in the coming chapters that includes:

- use of normative models that implicitly or explicitly root in comparison between teams and lead to a series of prescriptive *oughts* creates limited utility and likely has net negative effects on both us practitioners and the teams we support;
- utility, availability, relevance, and fit-for-use should be the primary criteria by which we assess OD scales, measures, and models from a Dialogic frame, rather than fixating on external validity, reliability, and predictability;
- a truly valuable inquiry process orients a team to engage in conversation, gain insights, become more self-aware, make meaning, gain agency, and chart their own definition of progress, all with our support rather than control. In so doing, we can put away the outside-in, N = big numbers studies, and rather focus on the N=1. *Their* inquiry and ownership of the results is aided by *our* focus on them;
- the role of the OD practitioner can shift in significant ways to account for the generative challenges accounted for in the

Dialogic mindset, particularly if we embrace a bias for pragmatic change with our clients. In so doing, our approach helps the team own its current situation, see themselves in their own multiple narratives, engage in meaningful inquiry, and move to action.

The implication of those assertions? The team's needs become very clear when we use the right lenses: empathy (not judgment); curiosity (not constrictive models); generative images and small, safe-to-fail experiments in which they quickly test and learn from the effectiveness of new approaches (not predictive or grand transformative efforts toward an idealized state); and a partner/coach who helps them find internal coherence and logic (not an expert OD assessor or auditor of performance).

The word "discover" in this book's title connotes in part a spirit of adventure, with a kinesthetic sense of hitting the open trail or sailing toward the boundless horizon. Deeper still, "discover" is meant to convey that our work with teams can be infused with an older, Middle English-use of the term: "to make fully known." This extends from how we help the team make itself known to itself and us, and how we ourselves become known to us and them.

How might all of this come together? A story will help. In chapter 1, I'll introduce you to a team coaching engagement with characters you might relate to. After that, in chapters 2 through 4, we'll pause our story to dive deep into the underpinnings of the Dialogic mindset, define our terms, compare and contrast the Diagnostic and Dialogic approaches, and delineate why the Dialogic approach offers advantages. We'll then return to our story for the remainder of the book in chapters 5–16 as we work through the engagement, pausing along the way to synthesize the *why*, *what*, and *how* of Dialogic team coaching. We'll close in chapter 17 with tentative conclusions and implications.

The offer, therefore, is to ride along on a brief coaching gig with Juliette and her leadership team. Join the OD practitioners, Ava and Orlando, who must navigate their own assumptions and pre-conditions to find emergent ways to support the team. Bring your best thinking and challenging questions to this gig, regardless whether you currently identify more as a Diagnostic or Dialogic OD professional, a leader looking for support, a team member, or a curious layperson. There's a seat right here at the table for you.

And help explore the eventual question: Just whose fish tank is it?

PART I

Context and Concepts

ONE

Diving In: Musing on a Fish Tank

We join the story here at what we, the external OD team, would consider the "beginning," although for the client team and its leader, it's just another day. Our bias suggests this is the start of something fresh and new; their bias suggests SS/DD...the "Same Stuff, Different Day."

Here's a quick introduction to our characters:

Juliette is a VP leader in a mid-size professional organization. The company recently went through a significant structural change, and the repercussions are being felt throughout hundreds of teams. Her experience is not at all unique, in that many other leaders are experiencing a profound discontinuity, awkward beginnings, even nostalgia for what had seemed to work well enough in the recent past. She likely is one of the few leaders to bring in outside support to help her and the team move forward.

Tom is Juliette's Program Manager and an important member of the team. He's responsible for tracking, managing, and reporting on all facets of their operation. For someone relatively early in his career, his bright eyes can't entirely mask the mix of sadness and resignation always running in the background of his experience. He is a no-nonsense driver, and he most values the shortest and most sensible path between two points.

Ava is the senior OD team member on the project. She met Juliette at a professional networking event, and early bonds of connection have blossomed into a formal project supporting Juliette and the team. Ava's 25 years of experience is varied, and one might think of her primarily as someone oriented toward a Dialogic OD mindset, which she weaves into the way she supports the team.

Orlando is the second OD team member on the project. He graduated with an MS in OD, which he's proud of. He's earlier in his career than Ava, and he's trying to build out a book of business with reference clients to help grow his budding practice. The opportunity to partner with Ava is significant. One might think of him primarily as someone oriented toward a Diagnostic OD mindset.

The **remainder of Juliette's nine-person team** arrives from different places in the wake of a reorganization, although it might be fair to sort them into at least two preexisting groups, as you will see. There is an assortment of compelling personalities, motivations, and histories that shape their interactions.

It is clear to everyone, especially herself, why Juliette has been in every Hi-Po program the company's L&D department ever offered. She is astute, intelligent, articulate, confident, and strategic, if not a bit too much so of all those attributes. If there were ever something important "going sideways" or out of control, Juliette would be one person you'd want to show up and bring order to the chaos, and look composed doing so. "Someday we'll all work for Juliette," is a phrase whispered more than once. But she knows that, of course.

Juliette graciously welcomes Ava into her office. "Ava, I've heard good things about how you've helped other teams in the past. My needs are pretty substantial, and I've got some amazingly fresh budget. I don't know what it is you do, but I'm all ears. Talk to me."

Not bothering to wait for an answer, Juliette purposefully strides across her office to a fish tank, brightly lit, bubbles bubbling. It's one small sign of life in the otherwise monotone, sterile, corporate environment. "Ava, this may be too much self-disclosure too soon, but I have to admit to you privately: when you make VP, there is absolutely zero training on how to lead a team of busy, strong-willed directors. I am mystified how some of my peers do it. How do they actually get people to collaborate? How do they get a team to feel, think, and act as a team...like, down deep? I have an idea that it's not by sending everyone to training. Taking the rare afternoon off to attend a sporting event and drink some beer creates a little good-natured conversation but almost nothing in terms of how to work together as a team. And is it too much for me to simply expect they'll work well together? Do I have to be in the middle of everything that happens?"

Juliette lifts the fish tank cover and, in a voice usually reserved for infants and pets says, "Hello, my friends!" Looking at Ava as the flakes hit the water, she explains "Just a bit of morning food for the few, simple beings I think I understand in this place. That clown fish...he's Romeo 17. He's had a few predecessors. The one sucking the green growth off the walls is Ted from Accounting. Sugar hides behind the rocks all day. Bunny is territorial and chases Big Red all over, Bistro eats and eats, I think because he's nervous..." Juliette's voice trails off, gazing into the tank.

"I'm curious," Ava says, leaning forward. "Reorganizations like the one you all just went through can really upset people. Does it look like things are finally settling out?"

"Hah! Great question, but you know the answer. I think we've reached some point of near-infinite complexity. Grant me some grace while I share my hard-earned cynicism. Confidential, right? These are things I'd simply never say to anyone else."

Ava nods.

"This new matrix structure locks everyone together into something unknown. At its best, it's a great way for this org to stay wired together. At its worst, it feels like some lattice of futility. Looking across my org and others, I just don't see how we'll ever get good at the collaboration required to make this new structure work. And when you look at my team—and I think this is the thing you might help us with—we simply do not communicate well. Those people sit in my conference room because my org chart now puts us together in a box, hinting at some potential synergy. But I can't yet see the necessary connections forming to make this structure come to life. Nada. Zip. Nothing."

Ava sits back. "It sounds like there's some co-existing mix of order and chaos. And that mix can leave one not knowing how to act. Or lead."

"Exactly. My instincts tell me that each one of these people is a wonderful person in their own right. They come from such different worldviews. They bring such unique constellations of strengths and weaknesses. And they have such different pressures in their personal lives. But that also means that there can be nine radically different views around the table about what's 'right' or 'good' or 'possible.' What in the world do you do with all that?"

"You're finding it can be hard to 'find the signal from the noise'?"

"That's a good way to put it. I want things to be different on my team, as it's the only place where we have a shot at taming the chaos. But when we finally take the time to talk about something important that we could change, we end up swirling. And the loudest voices too often win. We have some...how do I put it...interesting personalities on the team now."

Her shoulders sag a bit, as if the weight of the world had suddenly been tugged by an invisible force. "So, you're the expert. What do I do? I'm hoping you've got data and best practices that will help us cut to the heart of the matter in a pretty short period of time. Tell me you've got something up your sleeve. A roadmap to the path of least resistance: A list of 10 rules to follow. An infographic. A silver bullet maybe?"

Ava puts down her pen. "Juliette, your situation totally resonates with me. As much as I've heard it dozens of times, your telling of it catches me off-guard, particularly how people like you care so much and experience such great challenges. It seems like the crazy-making will never let up. You want the best for this team, and there's a lot at stake. But you feel ill-equipped, maybe not up to the task?"

"Yeah..." Juliette's eyes mist. This ounce of empathy feels like an ocean of compassion. Somebody understands me.

"I can safely guarantee you three things, Juliette. First, there is no other team like this one. It's radically unique in composition and context. There is no comparison to other teams or data sets that has any usefulness here. The only work we do together will be 100% relevant to this team. Things outside this team we will treat at best as tangential, and at worst as a distraction.

"Second, each person on this team has their own story about what's going on here. I'm going to help the team get the deepest insights about those stories as quickly as possible so that the team can find its own, shared 'signal from the noise.' It's only by taking this step that the team can create its own collective narrative about what is and what must be. This deep sense of shared ownership is vital to actually getting the outcomes you want in this complex environment.

"Finally, there is no 'silver bullet.' If there were, you would have already found it and used it, and we wouldn't be talking. The wisdom I can share, the process you and the team will go through, and the outcomes you all will achieve are totally predicted by your collective, courageous hard work, not wishful thinking. In the end, I will help equip you and the team to live in this world of near endless complexity, because that will never stop. Learning how to band together now and improve your shared effectiveness is something that pays dividends long after my time with you has ended.

"To answer your rhetorical question of a moment ago: Yes, at this point, it's too much to simply expect them to work well together. You can certainly hold each of them accountable for doing their job, but you're going to have to hold yourself accountable for helping them find the right points of collaboration and answer the Big Why: Why they should invest their time in this team. As leader, you'll have to help them explore and bring to life the space among them.

"One last question, maybe something we can talk about next time. That vibrant fish tank and the beautiful creatures you've put in it. So beautiful. But I'm curious...Whose tank is it? Yours...or Romeo 17 and his companions?"

Juliette stares out the window. A small smile returns to the corners of her mouth and her eyes brighten. "Right. Let's get started."

TWO

The Underpinnings of a Mindset

To prepare the ground for our comparison of Diagnostic and Dialogic approaches to team development, it's helpful to reacquaint ourselves with important contextual pieces of the mindset and paradigms that shape Dialogic thinking. Doing so will animate key distinctions and sow the seeds for the story that continues to unfold in Part 2.

What a wonderful world!

In 1967, Louis Armstrong recorded "What a Wonderful World." Its beloved lyrics describe, "skies of blue and clouds of white"; "friends shaking hands...saying, 'I love you'"; and babies who will "learn much more than I'll ever know." In these images plucked from daily life, Armstrong gives us the artist's gift of a simple picture of a wonderful world.

But viewed differently, just beyond these particularly simple images lies an equally wonderful, yet deeply *complex* world: why humans perceive the earth's atmosphere in the colors blue and white; how small groups of unaffiliated people can form bonds of trust and even convey abstract concepts, such as love, through simple, tactile interaction; how infants born today will have access to realms of information we cannot yet imagine, and how they will create useful knowledge from it.

As humans, we look at the world in many ways, both simple and complex. The song you write in life—be it simple or complex—turns on the ways you see and make meaning in the world. Our minds have limits on how much we can understand and incorporate, especially the very big (e.g., galaxies), the very small (e.g., subatomic particles), and the very complex or interrelated (e.g., social changes over generations). We tend to experience and describe complex patterns of events as discrete "things"— life, death, progress, failure, rush-hour traffic. We encapsulate them as infinitely simpler than they are. In reality, those things are rarely discrete events that follow a linear path or result from an identified or simple causal chain of events. Rather, they and we are woven in webs of ambient wonder.

Making sense of our daily interactions is done consciously and unconsciously through the construction of our personal, unique narrative about what's true and important in life, bounded by the limits of how we understand it. Each of our radically unique, constructed narratives is shaped by our histories and the world around us and given voice by the language we use.

Have you ever heard a team member describe their team as a "wonderful world?" It doesn't happen often (and maybe that should be one of our field's ultimate goals). Regardless, I am quite confident that in a team of nine, if we sat and listened to each person describe the image they hold in their mind of a wonderful team, or even just a pretty good meeting, we'd have nine different answers. As OD practitioners, what would *not* be relevant is your and my answer to that question to that team. It's their team, so it's their narrative, their sense to make, their coherence to establish, their collaboration to achieve, and their definition of effectiveness to live into.

It's their handshake saying *I love you.*

But how best to understand that? In this chapter we examine some of the underpinnings of the Dialogic mindset as applied to teams. Additionally, we briefly account for two situational factors of teams that shape our practice. First, in the always-on world of contemporary organizations, team members live in a state of what I'll call *attention poverty*, or the perpetual state of being in which competing claims for attention and prioritization outstrip team members' capacity to attend to those claims. The second is the near-infinite *diversity* of the people who live in teams, and thus by extension, the diversity and resulting uniqueness of each team.

Let's start there.

Uniqueness & Diversity

> *You've never quarreled with a fig tree because it doesn't bear cherries, have you?*
>
> —Nikos Kazantzakis, Zorba the Greek (1952)

Great strides have been made in recent years on topics related to organizational Diversity and Inclusion, or D&I. Diversity has centered on discernible or less discernible personal characteristics such as gender and gender identity; age and generation; sexual preference and orientation; disability and ability; socioeconomic status; and personality styles, to list a short subset. Inclusion has come to mean intentional strategies and tactics aimed at getting those diverse perspectives heard, experienced, understood, accepted, and utilized at different levels and places in the organization, and in a manner that actually includes all people in meaningful ways.

Without question, each individual is unique. While we share many human qualities, we are each incredibly different. When individuals are aggregated into teams, the diverse facets listed above no doubt come into play. In my experience, though, a much richer set of behavioral traits and personality dimensions are equally important and constantly at play in the day-to-day life of teams. When I enter a coaching relationship with a team and its leader, I most often hear about perceived differences that are causing conflict (rather than similarities that are creating alignment). Colloquially, some of those differences include:

- ability and readiness to trust others;
- conflict avoidance vs. comfort with, or desire for, conflict;
- varying ideas of what "success" means;
- being difficult to get along with (e.g., defiant, manipulative, bullying, or rigid) vs. relatively easy-going and graceful;
- oriented toward interdependence and collective outcomes vs. self-optimization;
- acting within established codes of behavioral or ethical conduct vs. being comfortable acting outside those bounds;
- highly competitive vs. less competitive;

- higher intelligence vs. lower intelligence, including emotional and social intelligence;
- higher levels of ambition vs. lower levels of ambition;
- engaged vs. disengaged attitudes toward work;
- highly reactive vs. deliberative and slow to act.

Moreover, beyond these personal traits, individuals bring both past and current situational life experiences to the team. Some important ones include:

- mental illness and substance abuse (per the Substance Abuse and Mental Health Services Administration, 2019, one in five American adults live with mental illness, one in 25 live with serious mental illness, 6.9% live with major depression, and 18.1% live with anxiety disorders);
- people who have been victims of significant trauma, such as sexual assault and domestic violence, who carry burdens of fear or shame;
- people who are in situations where extraordinary time and attention is demanded of them outside of the team, such as caring for sick or failing family members or being a new parent;
- people who experience their daily life in contemporary society through the general lens of ennui or even despair.

As Todd Rose brilliantly describes in The End of Average (2016), we're all walking different paths, embodying different traits, and using multi-dimensional talents to our best advantage. I'll extend that to say all of that is true in each and every *constellation* of individuals. Put simply, teams display immense compositional and contextual diversity because their members simply embody it. No one is really like anyone else, unless we apply over-generalizations and stereotypes.

Further, we can also acknowledge environmental and organizational factors that influence an individual's behavior within any given team. These, too, are legion, but a few important ones include:

- multiple, ongoing improvement or transformation initiatives;
- zero-sum game organizational performance management and compensation programs that amplify undue internal competition and individual optimization;

- matrix structures that challenge team members' abilities to work across functions, geographies, and processes;
- global teams that span multiple cultures, customs, languages, and time zones;
- organizations stressed by growth or downsizing.

Thus, each individual arrives at a unique team embedded in a specific context: its own time, place, and circumstances. They enter with some variant of an existing narrative of what it means to be a "good" team member. These existing narratives ride like source code in the background, and they're almost never intentionally revealed. Given this, in a team, it's fair to assume that people share a limited common narrative.

Our challenge? To embrace this kaleidoscope of past and present, assets and limitations, aspirations and constraints, and stories. Fear not: there is nothing here to be "tamed." There is nothing "wrong." It's a rich and wonderful world in many ways. Embracing this helps us become quiet and seek to understand before labeling someone an "independent variable" and imposing diagnostic criteria. Creating different "species" of teams as if they're in a zoo, categorizing them, labeling them, and managing them doesn't help. Narratives based on stereotypes, victimization, or demonization add nothing useful. Objectivity, to the degree it even exists, becomes less valuable to us than fascination and curiosity.

When we hold the truth of radically subjective individual diversity of capability and experience, it helps us advocate for the team's ability to create a shared language, meaning, and experience that enable collaborative work and the achievement of desired outcomes.

Complexity

> *...when we add people to the mix, we enter uncharted—and un-chartable—waters. The process becomes unavoidably complex.*
>
> —Chris Rodgers, Taking Organizational Complexity Seriously (2013)

In a crudely simplistic and perhaps not so *Wonderful World* view, a team is nothing more than a proximal group of rectangular boxes connected by lines in an org chart. A slightly more humanizing view might ask us to see a team as a bunch of people collected in a conference room, perhaps eating a pizza, or faces captured in a grid on a video call. But these perspectives strip teams of their humanity.

Similarly, OD practitioners have been socialized to see teams as always being at some stage in development, such as the wonderfully rhyming jingle of Form, Storm, Norm, Perform, Adjourn. Many of these models exist. They often say, "All teams must go through these stages on their journey to greatness." However, paradigms centered on developmental frameworks, while sometimes offering useful heuristic pictures of reality at the *macro* or aggregate scale, oversimplify the complexity of individual teams and their corresponding messiness.

Many solutions commercially available to teams focus on a simple *sum-of-their-parts* framework. This approach reduces living, breathing, wonderfully complex people to some set of individual personality characteristics and then aggregates them. Take your pick: MBTI types, DiSC profiles, Strengthsfinder, Insights, Enneagram. Having sat through too many of these to remember, I still cannot discern how, when all team members' results are put into a single mapping of results, it actually helps create a better team dynamic.

Quick surveys that take the team's "temperature" are well-meaning in a way that accentuates participative voice, and they provide a manager or team data of a sort. But knowing that "our energy is a 3.4 today while yesterday it was a 3.6" adds imperceptible value.

Many practitioners have been taught or unconsciously socialized to believe one can understand teams from a classical mindset, in which one can examine abstracted relationships and patterned causality, believing that they are true and universally applicable. But when this mindset is applied to teams and the ways we support them, it's devoid of wonder, curiosity, and a humanizing vibrancy that might inform our research and practice. (For outstanding theory and practice regarding complexity and uncertainty, see Eoyang's and Holladay's *Adaptive Action*, 2013.)

Our alternative, then, is to see the team as a living, breathing entity that:

- is comprised of unique individuals bonded in interdependence;
- often seeks or exists in a rough state of stability, regardless if that stability is experienced positively or negatively by members;

- intentionally or unintentionally finds minim
  from the chaos and rises to the level of mini
  effectiveness in pursuit of its ends;
- adapts to changes in its internal state and ext
  especially as those states and systems vacillat
  uncertainty;
- lives embedded in multiple external, complex
  simultaneously.

This complex adaptive system of a team never really perceives itself as one, if it perceives at all, just as I don't think of myself as an adaptive system when encountering a road closure due to construction while on the way to the grocery store. I likely go through some unconscious calculation and choose to either simply sit there and wait or find another route. I'm discerning the patterned or haphazard order and chaos in the environment to achieve my ends. My ability to get useful data about what roads are open and then adapt my strategy and tactics predicts my ability to eat dinner. Generally, I like to eat, so I'm pretty adaptive when something stands between me and food.

In the end, our job is to help the team and meet them where they're at. That may or may not include a discussion of complexity theory per se, but it can include helping them understand whether they're making it to *their* grocery store, nine people packed into a van, adapting to changes in their system. It can include helping them see the patterns in their internal experience and their external interfaces. It can include helping them establish or mend the vital pathways among one another that allow for coordination, collaboration, and emergent thought and action.

Narrative

> *We tell ourselves stories in order to live.*
>
> —Joan Didion (2006)

The most impactful people I know are skilled in giving their undivided attention in the moment to somebody who has something important to say (see Firth, 2020). This person can temporarily put aside analysis, comparison, or judgment and can access a certain unconditional

, compassion, and generosity. It's someone equipped with bal- openness, and really beautiful questions.

There is a rare, tangible comfort and intimacy in being heard and understood by someone else in this way. Our story, which even we so often struggle to make sense of, becomes an object of wonder. Our experience, which is so often minimized, is affirmed. Our assumptions, hidden in the shadows, emerge for self-inspection. The self's mirror materializes, and our courage to gaze into it emerges. The potential for change—even transformation—becomes something greater than zero.

In teams, we each bring stories shaped from past experiences. Those stories are transfigured over time by our retellings, our selective memories, and our fantasies. We rely on them, unaware. Importantly, we create narratives *together*. Our shared experiences over time are laid down like the layers of a fine lasagna. Our shared understandings of common experiences are like some jostled Venn diagram of sub-narratives, wholly imperfect and misshapen, yet unique and valuable, intertwined in our joined experience and expression. "Ah, so THAT'S what a 'team player' is supposed to do in *this* organization. Did you see what she did there? That was *so* impactful."

Our understanding of these stories is often limited to the discrete, surface things seen in artifacts, such as spreadsheets with budgets, presentations with plans, or the late night hours at which we leave the office. The deeper meanings, as there are many, lies out of reach in the crush of daily life until the ***listener*** shows up. With simple, compelling questions, the anthropologist's eye, the heart of a confidant, the patience, attention, and commitment of a sculptor, the listener sits in the crucible with the teller.

It's hard to be a listener for others when we quietly mentally process what we hear as "she's a Type II" something, or "they're in some stage of Norming," or "I bet 85% of people on this team will say the same thing." Activating the evaluative part of our brain that orients toward assessment, comparison, and prediction subjugates the part of our mind that is required for fostering deep insights and making meaning, be it with an individual or a team.

When we pick our mindset, we pick the story we hear and the path we walk on with the team. Both Dialogic and Diagnostic paths offer value, but they bring a qualitatively different focus and fuel. They foster different experiences. I've never seen a spreadsheet or model of team development bring a tear to the eye, but I've seen people weep in a team when they feel heard and understood on visceral topics. When their narrative is given voice, they become more curious about others' narratives. And the table is set for insights not previously possible.

Can the team use these narratives, once uncovered, as an organic asset to create coherence? Absolutely. The path to finding the utility of narrative is through attending and close listening. A question to ponder, then: is part of our role in a Dialogic frame to help team members acquire listening skills and apply them in their daily lives? If narrative is key, then without some minimum viable listening, how can the team find its path forward together?

In that way, we might extend Joan Didion's quote above to "We tell ourselves stories in order to live...and we tell each other stories and give each other the gift of listening in order to live *together*."

Attention poverty

> *Sure, we've got lots of time for this fairly in-depth work. We're excited to do it in a way that honors a much more deliberative pace of conversation that leads to mutual understanding, aligned action, and mutual support. I want to relax into this over the next months.*
>
> —No client ever

The construct of "team" has been on the rise for decades. I don't think my parents were on as many teams in their entire careers as I was on in a single year as a VP in a large organization. According to Google Ngram the use of the word team in print in the USA has gone up 1,186 percent since 1900; it now shows up almost every 10,000 words.

Over time, I've anecdotally collected information from speaking and coaching engagements where I usually ask people the same three questions:

- Between work and home, how many teams are you on? (Average answer is nine.)
- What percentage of those teams would you say meets your personal threshold for being *effective* or *highly effective*? (Average answer is 15–20%.)
- What percentage of the teams that are *not* effective, that is, the 80–85%, get any measure of support? (Average answer is <5%.)

Diagram 1: How often the word team shows up in print between 1900 and 2008

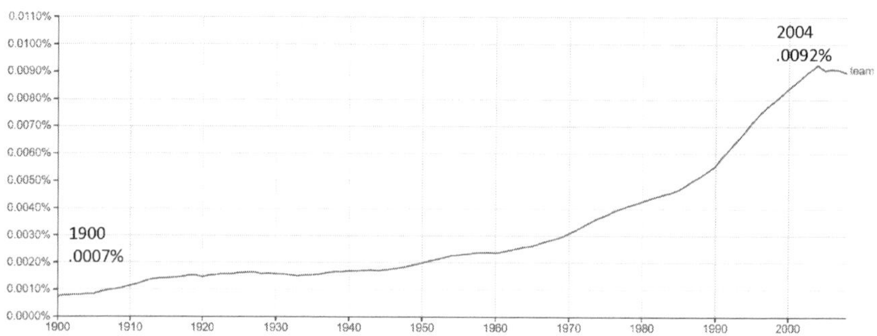

Adapted from Google Books Ngram viewer, March 2020

If your car started only 20% of the time, or if your mobile phone carrier company gave you an ineffective 1-bar signal 80% of the time, you'd quickly look for alternatives. And still, we mindlessly put people into teams, earnestly believing that we don't need to stop for a moment and ask if "one more team" added to the mix will be a problem, a panacea, or a paradise. Or further, how we maximize the ROI of that "team."

Years ago, I was coaching a VP and her team at a global manufacturing company. She had been given a talking point for the all-hands meeting by a direct report, the leader of the quality function, about how "attending to quality was everyone's job and should be everyone's #1 priority." Watching her presentation, I saw eyes glaze over. The marketing director mustered a solemn nod of assent.

After the meeting, I asked the VP what she thought about that brief moment. "I'm just being a good corporate citizen," she mumbled, annoyed by my focus on such an inconsequential part of an already too-difficult day. I nudged further. "How many #1 priorities do you think these leaders have?" "I have no idea," she said with mild frustration. "Why don't you go count them up for me."

So, I did. I went back and reviewed a year of messaging to the team. I wrote a one-page overview of everything that had been referenced as a top priority. No doubt you can name a number of them: quality; safety; living the values; being a brand ambassador; fiscal responsibility; hitting your goals; getting closer to the customer; developing the next level down managers; even, letting your people experience you as a "real person." I closed the brief overview and long list with the simple statement, "When everything is a priority, nothing is. This makes everyone numb."

Beyond that, people are also wearied by all that from the world of HR and OD we well-meaningly foist on them: engagement surveys and follow-up plans; performance management and rewards processes; compliance training; manager development; recruiting efforts; even the latest faddish expectation that leaders take selfies with their organization's members and post them on social media. Sigh.

The people who populate today's organizations—and their teams—are in a perpetual state of attention poverty. The causes are endemic, and we tilt at windmills to change them. In decades of coaching teams, I've not had a client voice the faux quote at the top of this section. In the kick-off meetings of clients I engage with, someone usually courageously gives voice to what many people invariably feel: "there is just *no way* I can dedicate the hours you're asking for to work on this team and its effectiveness." I congratulate the person who says it. Voicing their reality is an act of openness fueled by safety and trust. It's an act of ownership.

Over years, team members' adaptive response to increasing environmental pressures is to develop a highly refined BS detector. They can sniff out useless platitudes before they fall from our lips. They know when their leader has grabbed onto an external consultant or coach like a life preserver. They can play-act flawlessly, nodding their head that, indeed, *this is important*, while they silently figure out how to catch up on their real work/day job, now hopelessly behind due to this team offsite.

To engage with an intact team and leader is to be swept into their voice, their pace, their conflicting demands, their constraints, and soon, their fears and aspirations. Exhausted people have heightened distractibility, decreased patience, less optimism, and greater limits on their learning.

What's the impact of that on our work? We become duty bound to show them the relevance of the work they'll do with us without promising outcomes, which are totally unknowable. We have the responsibility to help them understand their opportunity to own this work, if they so choose, and the probabilistic benefits of being increasingly more adaptive to the complex world around them.

There are many perceived constraints to this type of work. Most often cited is money. "There just isn't budget for this" is a common refrain.

The second is time. "There just aren't enough hours in the day to do this." All true statements. In the end, I believe the scarcest and most fragile enabler of their effectiveness is their *attention*, and the behaviors that fuel attention: *focusing* and *prioritization*.

Our teams live at the nexus of near infinite demands and near infinite constraints. That makes our work with them likely to be challenged in execution and often limited in impact. To lead client teams off in a directionless investigation of narrative and complexity is to challenge their goodwill. We ourselves must adapt. Equipping them with efficient yet effective meaning-making constructs, giving them a reasonable chance to understand and improve their daily lives, and doing so without confining them to predictive models, well, that's important and intriguing work.

THREE

Defining Terms and Comparing Mindsets

My views on the underpinnings of the Dialogic mindset described above set the stage for us to look at the heart of the matter: How do Diagnostic and Dialogic paradigms (Bushe & Marshak, 2014) compare when supporting teams? What might lead one to believe that the Dialogic mindset offers both unique advantages and challenges in today's complex world? Through which set of lenses should we view the work at hand, particularly as it plays out in our story in chapters 5–16?

Discovery awaits.

A dark road.

Imagine: The road before you darkens as dusk settles in the snow-dusted hills. This has always been your family's favorite driving trip with your close friends and their children. Two cars full of laughter, music, and the feelings that accompany adventure and long-awaited downtime. With sunset, temperatures have drifted down near freezing, and the nascent moon flickers on frost starting to form on leaves scattered by the creek next to the road.

You check your rearview mirror to see your friend's car a safe distance behind you. The two cars ahead are other unknown travelers on this stretch of road, strangers in every sense. It's easy to hypnotically follow their taillights through the curves and watch their headlights illumine the road ahead. It's fun to be in the flow, these four vehicles connected as if on a rollercoaster. The miles slip by. Soon it's been 20 minutes since you've passed the diffuse glow of city lights.

A clear and disconcerting thought enters your mind: those headlights from the lead car are starting to illumine…the trees above…and now the creek below. Chaos emerges first for you the driver, as the car directly in front of you skids to a halt.

The first car clearly went off the road. *Was it the frost? An animal? Maybe a tired driver? We should check on them.* Your friends in the car behind have likewise stopped, and quickly they're standing on the roadside next to your open window. The expressions on their faces mirror what you're feeling and thinking: fear, concern, urgency. Chills creep up the back of your neck, partly from the adrenaline and partly from the shock of cold air.

As you approach the sedan now resting 90 degrees on its side in the creek, it doesn't make sense that a car in knee-deep water should be on fire. The smoke from the engine is acrid, burning your eyes and nose. Your partner, peering in through the front window, says that there's a single driver plus two young children in the back seat. The driver appears very severely injured, but the children seem safely bundled in car seats.

The driver from the car immediately in front of you, a slight young woman with an Asian accent, assesses the situation. She makes clear the only way to get the passengers out will be for someone to climb atop the car, break the passenger window, climb in, and lift the children out.

"I'll do it," she says. "You, call emergency. Someone get me a tire iron. Something I can break the window with." She looks you in the eye with a focused calmness: "Give me a hand so I can climb up there. The smoke is getting thick. We got this. *We* have got this. Help me up. NOW."

You have no idea who the woman is, but you trust her. And, those on the scene are all these kids have to help them survive. You intertwine your fingers and offer her a place to step up onto the car and into the task at hand.

Describing key concepts

> *Interdependence is and ought to be as much the ideal of man as self-sufficiency.*
>
> *Man is a social being.*
>
> —Mahatma Gandhi

To be true to our commitment to explore teams through a Dialogic lens, we must commit to inhabit the worlds they live in. To create focus, we must fixate on the team as a unit of analysis, and at least at this point, focus on neither the broader organization writ large nor the individual actor. It's this smaller social ecosystem that is the subject of our inquiry. When I say "**team**," I am broadly including all manifestations of smaller social ecosystems in which there is:

- **membership** (a *we* that is known);
- **purpose** and **core responsibilities** (a discernible *why*, *what*, and *how*);
- **interdependence** among members necessary for the team to accomplish its ends (a shared agreement that we will succeed *only if* we to some degree rely on one another);
- sufficient **permanence** (a reasonable *stability* over time, given the purpose).

Return for a moment to the opening scene in the prior section. Using this definition, the three carloads of people who pull to the side of the road are definitely a team. There is some sense of membership (it's just us), a purpose to the work (we have to get the kids out) and an idea of how best to do that, a reliance on others to accomplish the ends (if you help me up onto the car...), and some sense that no one is going to drive away before the task is accomplished. What is *not* more important than the task at hand includes knowing each other's name, MBTI type, vision for how this work might go, sense of shared identity, measures of success, or motivation.

Teams take almost any size and shape. I make some assumptions about our shared experiences of being on teams in organizations, and I list those here, as they form the basis for much of what's explored in the mindset foundational to Dialogic team development. They include:

- organizations have adopted teams as the predominant way of organizing productive effort;
- organizations are immensely complex in multiple dimensions, which often encourages people to adopt an external locus of control or belief they are subject to outside events and forces, rather than an internal belief that they can shape their world;

- people become resigned that their situation cannot change, and that it's often easier to keep their head down than attend to their team's effectiveness;
- individuals consequently often lead lives of alienation in organizations;
- people become suspicious, resistant, and resentful of attempts to "change them" for the better.

You will note that up to this point, I've rarely used the term "**leader**," which connotes a position of authority over the team. This is intentional. In our examination of teams, I portray the leader *as but one member of the team, albeit an incredibly important one. They are part of the systemic entity called "team."* The leader's effectiveness is intrinsically tied to the team's effectiveness. The leader's development takes place within the team ecosystem. They are one. For clarity, think of "team+leader" or "leader+team" each time I say "team."

By "**team effectiveness**," I mean each team's collective ability *to establish enough of what they need in order to accomplish their ends, regardless of changing conditions.* If one team needs clarity around responsibilities, their effectiveness will increase to the degree they can create that clarity. If another team needs a better way to surface and resolve conflict, then their effectiveness will be enhanced to the degree they can do that. I make few, if any, assumptions that a team must have something *a priori* in order to function as a team.

The team's unique context, composition, unfolding narrative, particular strengths and weaknesses, and everything else we may or may not notice shape what is needed to help the team engage in inquiry as to how to improve its effectiveness.

Comparing mindsets

It may be helpful to have a brief but more crystallized description of some of the ways in which Diagnostic and Dialogic OD differ when it comes to teams. These generalizations are loose, and I offer them as a means to an end: to begin to highlight how these different facets show up in the ebb and flow of a supportive engagement.

The long-established Diagnostic approach to supporting teams is often based on a set of assumptions. For example, these assumptions typically include:

- the practitioner is an expert in assessing teams and guiding their development;
- teams transition between normal or expected development states (e.g., Form-Storm-Norm-Perform-Adjourn), often linearly portrayed;
- data derived from studies of large numbers of teams can be applied in a normative manner back to individual teams;
- OD-centric values and definitions of terms position us to advocate for what's "good" for a particular team (e.g., "you need a more democratic process") without understanding if that value brings a perceived good within the unique, socially constructed narrative and cultural context of that team.

Table 1 below highlights distinctions between Diagnostic and Dialogic OD when looking at the role of the OD practitioner. Distinctions are easy to see when contrast is high and differences stark. They're less easy to see when nuanced. These two tables push the contrast to accentuate the difference. You, the reader, will have your own interpretation whether the differences are as stark as I've posed. Given the wonderful diversity of OD practitioners at work, you may see these quite differently.

Table 1: Diagnostic and Dialogic viewpoints about the role of the OD Practitioner

Factor	Diagnostic Orientation	Dialogic Orientation
Role of the OD practitioner	A consultant who can help solve a technical problem with reliable models and valid data	A coach who is intrinsically embedded in the process to help the team discover its current narrative and path forward
Best practices	Can be found externally and applied across and within teams	Can be found or interpreted internally within the team
Process owner	OD directs or cocreates the process	The team+leader has agency to own the process together
Relies on support mechanisms such as...	Surveys based on models of optimal team characteristics and training-oriented solutions that fill competency gaps	Processes of inquiry that produce emergent, low-risk experimentation without expectation of what will happen

Factor (cont)	Diagnostic Orientation (cont)	Dialogic Orientation (cont)
Practitioner tools	Extensive toolbox with best practice–based remedies to fill identified gaps, often with *external* case studies	Extensive toolbox with constant adaptation to the team's evolving language and emergent, complex needs, often using generative modes of dialogue
Takes comfort in	Data and clear process that deliver on project commitments	Supporting emergence in each unique team instance
Draws from paradigms in	Science of management Social psychology Organization behavior	Anthropology Counseling psychology Postmodern social sciences Complexity science

Table 2 highlights distinctions between Diagnostic and Dialogic OD when looking at the intervention or inquiry process itself.

Table 2: Diagnostic and Dialogic viewpoints about the OD intervention or support process

Factor	Diagnostic Orientation	Dialogic Orientation
Assessment	External; expert (or leader) centric	Team self-inquiry
Data	Objective, normative	Subjective, ipsative
Measures	Precise, unbiased measures with external validity and reliability	Imprecise, necessarily biased measures with internal validity and utility
Understanding is achieved through	Aggregation of team member's abstracted viewpoints (e.g., average scores on surveys)	Shared, subjective meaning making
Model	Most commonly one of three approaches: 1. Linear, developmental, or expressed in a capability maturity model 2. Causal Input-Process-Output models 3. Aggregation of individual characteristics (e.g., MBTI, DiSC, Insights, et al.)	Non-linear, holistic, and systems-thinking, with no predefined entry points or pre-set indicators for what "progress" means Holds notions of what parts of the system should be attended to

Factor (cont)	Diagnostic Orientation (cont)	Dialogic Orientation (cont)
Comparison across teams	Possible and helpful; leads to labeling teams within given constructs (e.g., type of team, development stage, type of dysfunction)	Impossible and perhaps not helpful; instead validates the team's right to use its own language to understand itself and its progress
Role of theory	Inductive or deductive, in that through research, principles are derived and generalized from studies of teams, and then those principles are applied back to other individual teams	While models can help create useful lenses, any prescriptive theory of how a team *should be* is less useful when applied to the unique exigencies of a single team
Developmental activities rooted in...	Idealized image of a "good" or "healthy" team. A proscribed path and planned activities are offered along a linear model; less customized, more defined activities rooted in the planned change	Probabilistic opportunities for insight-driven change, with flex based on constant emergence to different states of being and capability, optimally toward greater effectiveness; no set starting point or ending point Highly customized to address unique, *in situ*, perceived needs within the shared narrative

At its heart, diagnosis is a process rooted in distinguishing and determining which malady best explains the signs reported and symptoms observed. It requires an expert observer, a subject to observe, models that create theoretical consistency, and measures and data that aid discernment. Diagnosing a team brings to bear all that: our expertise in team theory; our role in distinguishing their malady; their pain or suboptimal process or state; our models, measures, and data; their reliance on us for prognosis and prescription.

Moving forward, we need to examine the potential implications of the differences we find between the two mindsets and further, *how the Dialogic paradigm equips us to engage in the process of coaching a team.* How does the Dialogic mindset shape what an OD practitioner might decide as wise and constructive action?

FOUR

A Case for the Dialogic Path Forward

All models are wrong, some are useful.

—attributed to George Box, statistician (1976)

Can a new pair of lenses in our goggles help us view and support teams in a different way? Seeking Dialogic understanding places us in a different role. Impact is created at the intersection of emergence, adaptation, experimentation, and resilience. But before moving to our story of application, we should explore the implications of the different mindsets and concretely lay out the beliefs that shape how our practice takes shape. We should consider how certain facets fade to the background, while others move to fore.

Ownership

When we orient toward the internal meaning-making of individuals and teams and shift away from a reliance on external reference points, we're left with an unsettling realization: the most important things are *inside* the team, not *outside* it. The people in the team are the only ones with the right and responsibility to change the interior landscape of their experience.

In general, we take better care of things we believe we own rather than things we rent. We don't wash and wax rental cars before returning them at the airport. Pride of ownership connotes attending, caring, and supporting. If team members can see that *only they* own their team experience, they position themselves to develop an internal locus of control.

When we enter their space with them, we come with our own narratives, histories, scars, and aspirations. We arrive with our mental models and data, our case studies and embarrassments, our blind spots and foibles. We own *those* things.

In the moments we are with them inside their system, we are part of the shared meaning making and search for coherence. But the quest is fundamentally theirs. Being explicit in that ownership is key in Dialogic OD team coaching.

Paths toward the end in mind

The team's search for coherence in a complex world is a never-ending journey. From stasis comes change, from chaos, order, and vice versa. The team's challenge in these conditions is to find *adaptable paths to greater effectiveness,* rather than some rarified state of a pinnacle, high-performing team. Their ability to survive and thrive in a complex world, to learn from novel experience, to discern patterns and make good guesses, to deliver on their charter and demonstrate an ROI for the resources afforded them is not done by achieving a certain anointed status, but by striving for a state of effectiveness commensurate to the undulating challenges within and among them.

The scourge of comparison

"I was once on this phenomenal leadership team," offered a potential client. "I want you to help me recreate that team experience here." His request, a plea really, was to engage with him in the impossible. While having a phenomenal team experience is a too-rare experience, it's also not replicable.

I replied, "Your experience at that company was what it was, in that setting, with those people, with those forces at play. None of that exists here, only you and the narrative you carry about what a great team experience usually is. And even *you* are not the same as you were then. I'm afraid I can't help you compare this team to that team. What is possible is to engage *this* team in a conversation about how they uniquely could be a phenomenal team by their own definition and in their own right."

Diagnosis always involves comparison, and despite the fact that we're very good at it, there's a long list of things we shouldn't compare between teams, given the radically unique composition and context of each team. These include their current performance and what enables or detracts from it; strengths and weaknesses; potential; developmental needs; and solutions that might offer a path forward.

Comparison also has some important downsides to it:

- **Comparison is always limiting**, as any comparison contains within it the seeds of its own failings, as the unique entities being compared will never be identical in composition and context.
- **Comparison encourages a sense of relative deprivation.** It might well be that from our outside perspective, a particular team lacks something, say, a commitment to a singular purpose. However, this might not be in any way true for the team members themselves. They simply exist in their natural state. Highlighting that *compared to other teams, we feel they're missing something* creates in them not only the incrementally new sense of missing something but also the embarrassment that they were not aware enough to know they were missing something.
- **Comparison can create deficit thinking**, and it can foster the search for blame or useless envy.
- **Comparison distracts teams from focusing *inside***, where important work is to be done, toward focusing *outside*, to imaginary other teams or aggregations. If we compare a team to a sample set of 1,000 teams, or a honeybee hive, or a pod of dolphins, we've taken their mind away to things they cannot truly understand, and likely poorly imagine.
- **Comparison can warp motivation**, in that it can create feelings of inferiority or superiority, whether or not those are valid or useful.
- **Comparison can breed competition** between teams where none is warranted

In short, **comparison is the thief of joy.**

That's not to say outside images and metaphors have no place in the team's discussion of an aspirational future state. Imagine a team member says, "I wish we were more like a pride of lions." One might reply, "OK, what behaviors or beliefs do you imagine reside in a pride of lions that makes them effective *together*?" And then, "How would you like to see those beliefs and behaviors manifest in this team?" And then, "What part of the lion inside you is ready to believe and behave that way?" In that sense, the pride of lions forms a generative image, at least for one person. This piece of comparative narrative could be richly explored. But for us to evaluatively say, "I've seen better intentionality in slime mold," well, that is not likely to help.

The proper use of comparison in a team is in t*he team members' assessment of their progress over time.* In this, the team could describe their current state of effectiveness, including the drivers of that state, to the recent past. In this comparison, the team's internal variables are likely stable (e.g., composition, context), and the new current state may have been realized because of their ownership of, and intentional focus on, improving a few key drivers. It's useful to compare the "us" of *then*, the "us" of *now*, and the hoped-for "us" of soon-to-be. It's not useful to compare the "us" of now with some other team, real or idealized, of a different composition and context.

When my wife and I were pregnant with twins, we received a sage piece of advice. "You'll be tempted to compare them. Who learned to crawl first...who is a better sleeper...who is better at math. Just don't. It's not fair to them, and it's a bit lazy. Treat them like the wonderful individuals they are, each on their own terms."

There's good reason to do the same with our teams.

Measures and models

The philosophical underpinnings of Dialogic OD discussed thus far open the door for us to create alternatives in how we help the team describe and understand its effectiveness. While Diagnostic OD grounds itself in the clinical precision of management science and orients toward the rigors of variables and validity, Dialogic OD claims the latitude to move away from that precision and rigor.

If we are not in the business of comparing teams, and if we're willing to accept each on its own terms, we can give greater import to the richness of description and the utility the data offers the team. That's not to say that data itself has no importance. It's an efficient means by which we help the team members explore their narrative and chart a path forward. Rather, from a Dialogic OD frame, we have choices in the data collected, who does so, what it describes, and what gets done with it. **Our *intent* shifts.** This might be best described as choosing a trowel rather than a scalpel, or choosing broader, looser, yet internally valid and relevant sources of data from which the team derives its insights. This shows up in at least two important ways.

First, the **measures** we use do not need to be grounded in objective and normative data. Rather, we can reorient ourselves toward a subjective understanding of internal experience through *ipsative* measures that matter most to team members. For example, in ipsative assessments, the individual is directed to choose among generally positive characteristics without using scales to rate traits. This can be contrasted against *normative* assessments in which the individual uses a scale, such as a Likert scale of 1 to 7, to rate selected characteristics.

Here's an example of a simple ipsative question:

> *Which one of these statements most accurately reflects your view? Choose only one:*
>
> *A. I find it easy to participate openly in team conversations*
> *B. This team has a good understanding of its purpose*

This type of assessment provides no springboard for diagnosis, other than it begins to create a data set around each person's experience and the value they ascribe to those experiences. If six of nine team members chose answer A, it would be fascinating to hear *why* individuals chose their answer, and even more interesting what the team makes of this resulting discussion. But what we have *not* done is found out that on a scale of 1 to 7, this team rates its Clarity of Purpose a 3.2, nor have we further compared that result to other, more "highly effective teams," who consistently rate Clarity of Purpose a 5.2.

These types of looser, less precise, and more subjective measures might be new for some, but they're not altogether unfamiliar constructs. We often encounter them in daily life.

- When you go to a medical facility and a nurse asks, "What's your pain on a scale of 1 to 10?" and shows you the Wong-Baker Faces Pain scale, you're using a loose, subjective scale to judge your pain at this moment against all the pain you've ever felt and all the pain you might imagine feeling. It doesn't matter how anyone else rated abdominal pain that day, or how most people with appendicitis assess their pain score. What matters is how *you* rate the pain, and if it's better or worse than a few hours ago.

- When you leave an airport restroom and there is a small electrical pod where you can rate the cleanliness of the bathroom using three faces, from frowny to smiley, you're using a loose, subjective scale. You are not measuring the number of bacteria per cubic centimeter on the sink and comparing it to all airport bathrooms. You are simply saying, "Frowny face, because I think this place is a mess."
- In bicycling-centric personal training, Power Zone training allows each person to compete against their own recent performance using their subjective basis for effort. Rather than engaging in objective time or intensity trials against other people, you act as your own competition, and what matters is growth over time against your own standards of performance.

Diagnostic OD team surveys often anchor into broad collections of data gleaned from large populations of teams, which inform supposed normative standards, which are then re-applied back to an individual team. Anchoring in normative data fosters correlations that seed predictions about what might help a team improve. Critically, it's this *reapplication of norms and correlation (posing as causation) back to the single team* wherein the problems lie, as there is fallacious reasoning here.

To say, "A study of 1,500 leadership teams shows that mistrust is the number one predictor of poor team performance," and then by extension, "Therefore, I think *this* particular team should work on its trust," is to engage in the Ecological Fallacy. The Ecological Fallacy occurs when one makes a conclusion about a particular individual team from an analysis of a large group of teams. For example, if you studied 100 leadership teams at large not-for-profit organizations and concluded that their consistent key strength was "clear purpose," and then you had the chance to work with a single, demographically similar team in a similar setting elsewhere, it would be fallacious to conclude that one of their strengths was "clear purpose." One cannot apply a generalized conclusion to a specific individual, full stop. To do so is to commit the Ecological Fallacy. To even imagine it creates bias and expectation, conscious or unconscious.

Therefore, by putting aside this kind of normative data, we are free to look at *any* vital characteristics that help individuals describe themselves and the team, including both qualitative and quantitative data, with varying degrees of subjectivity. You will see how this might be done in the upcoming chapters that continue our extended story.

Second, **models** originating from a Diagnostic frame come encumbered with assumptions about how teams work. As stated in the quotation above, all models are wrong, but some are useful. They're all necessarily wrong because the world is more complex than any model could ever account for. Many team models over the decades have offered a view of teams grounded in causality, linearity, and the never-ending climb toward "great team" status (often described as capability maturity models). These models get great uptake, as they give clients a sense of contained exploration, predictable outcomes arising from effort, and a validated goal to attain. For practitioners, they help us portray our diagnostic expertise. "I can help you get from Stage 2 to Stage 3."

One other particular variant on these themes is the aggregation of personality characteristics that form some sort of topology of differentness. Perhaps half the team members are extroverts, half introverts. Or some percentage of us are oriented toward dominance in interaction, while a significant portion are oriented toward conscientiousness. In this approach, it's believed that understanding the *constellations of difference* creates insights team members can handily use in interaction. While there is, no doubt, value in understanding aspects of difference *within* each person, this approach fails to address the space *among* people and the important dynamic that unfolds, often beyond our ability to describe it. Rather than knowing two team members are conflict avoidant, might it not be more interesting and useful to explore what unfolds among us all when conflict isn't resolved? Rather than knowing five team members sense above-average psychological safety, might it not be more valuable to know if a sense of safety and trust is felt needed or missing by team members? Might it not be richer to understand how Beethoven's Fifth Symphony makes you feel than to count the number of notes and rests on the score?

Team models from a Dialogic frame can offer multiple points of entry without buying into assumptions of linearity and causality. They can offer insights into the deeper patterns of interaction *within* and *among* team members that help teams get enough of what they need in order to be effective, rather than imposing a prescribed, constraining, or irrelevant worldview into their complex lives.

As humans, we understand and model our universe in a way that simplifies and abstracts it into a form we can digest. The path we offer the team can bring accurate enough pictures of the complex world at play, along with reasonable simplicity, such that a team can use it to construct a shared narrative. This approach to modeling offers maximal utility.

Pragmatism

If we jettison our Diagnostic models of "greatness" and the corresponding metrics that help us compare, it can leave us feeling adrift. At the same time, the sweeping, changing vistas of postmodern social construction of narrative embedded in the theoretical underpinnings of Dialogic OD, might challenge our ability to help the team find its most important things to work on. Where can we anchor? We anchor into the team, its experience, and changes they might make to improve their effectiveness as they strive to collaborate in interdependence.

Pragmatically, it is better to seek just a few, critical variables to help the team attend to *not* because our model or data say so, but because their own inquiry and quest for coherence demands it. Their claiming a set of priorities, with our support and reflection, is a fundamental act of ownership. We coach the team and leader as an intact system as it searches for temporal coherence in a too often crazily complex system embedded in a dynamic, constantly changing world.

Helping diverse team members find their voice and express their narrative in the team's joint construction of a shared narrative is possible without edging toward the chaos of too many voices. We can help them focus on just a few important elements based on *their* wisdom. The design principle of equifinality suggests that there are many paths to any desired end. We can help them trust the process such that no matter where they start, their journey of discovery will bring them to their most useful place of self-improvement.

As they progress down the path of pragmatic improvement, we can be the teacher that "appears" as the student becomes focused and "ready" for new stretches in their development. As needs emerge, we stand ready with a rich and wonderful toolbox, customizable to their unique means and ends. The trust we need to build is not that we will diagnose precisely or remediate expertly, but that we will help them reflect on themselves and then bring to bear an array of tools to help the team make the progress *they* deeply desire in the most pragmatic, efficient manner possible.

A bridge to application

A fluid, reciprocally influenced relationship between the client and practitioner shapes the work we do together. *Our* assumptions about measures and models set *them* on a course of sense-making. Their complex interworking and adaptation to externalities might fit well within our preconceived models, or they might not. Tensions within those ebbs and flows often influence project and team success, and they merit our attention. In the end, **our job is to help them find their idea of an effective team, not limit them to our idea of a team.**

In pursuit of this, when lightening our hold on the Diagnostic mindset, we may be tempted in frustration to say, "Well, then, throw it *all* away!" But I don't actually think that's required. Orienting toward pragmatism rather than purity tests, we can simply face the challenge of asking ourselves: If our current Diagnostic models and measures don't do the job for us in this brave new world, what might? What awaits our experimentation? Is there a creative way to bring the very best of Diagnostic along with us on our Dialogic journey? Similarly, we may grow cautious or weary of Dialogic's seeming squishiness, the perceived absence of an objective and abstract standard, or the sense that there are no tools for proper measuring. What to do?

Our path forward emerges by extending Robert Quinn's (2004) metaphor "Building the bridge as you walk on it." Our role is to help the team+leader explore the bridge to a future they desire. This might involve helping them sketch a design, find a tree, saw a branch, hew a board, nail it to possibly unsteady supports, and then tentatively step on it together. And then do it again. And again. This definition of emergent help demands our courage, and it produces calloused hands, both theirs and ours.

What awaits us, then, is the sawdust of bridge building.

PART TWO

Entry and Contracting

I get those fleeting, beautiful moments of inner peace and stillness—and then the other 23 hours and 45 minutes of the day, I'm a human trying to make it through in this world.

—Ellen DeGeneres (2001)

As OD practitioners Ava and Orlando begin their exploration of the life of the team, they must navigate two important contracting conversations. First, given that they've not worked together before, they must begin to understand each other's Dialogic and Diagnostic perspectives on the work and how to proceed. Their interactions over time will be part ballroom dancing, where one person leads and another follows, part line dancing with highly choreographed, synchronized moves, and part mosh pit, where an emergent, bouncing energy takes over.

Second, they must establish a healthy working partnership with Tom, Juliette's Program Manager. He is the undisputed gatekeeper to the team's time and focus, and the initial conditions they create with him will shape the initial conditions for the project.

FIVE

Two Mapmakers

Ava leads the way as she and Orlando navigate a tight path to the only open table in the far corner of the crowded coffee shop. "It's great to have you joining me on this project, Orlando. It's fun to work with new people. I always learn a lot."

"Me too, Ava," he says as they settle in. "I understand some of the people in our network consider your approach to this team development work..."

"Different?"

"Yeah, different. I don't know if that means better or worse. I'm interested to see where our approaches are similar and where they vary."

Ava nods. "Let's dig in. I want to share with you my notes from my initial conversation with the client team leader, Juliette. She's got a lot going on. But let's begin by sharing with each other how we usually frame this work from an OD perspective. I'm really curious to hear your thoughts. How do you usually start a project like this?"

"I'd start by saying that I'm a social scientist at heart. I so enjoyed the classes I took in grad school that trace the development of OD over the last decades. The giants' shoulders we stand on have brought us to such a position of strength when we look at their models, the creation of normative data...just their mindset and their pursuit of a science of OD."

"Totally agree. It's been hugely valuable to our field. How does all that show up for you with a client, say, when you're coaching or consulting with them?"

"I think it's useful to gather valid data on the team and then help them quickly compare where they're at developmentally with other teams. Do they know their mission, vision, and goals? If not, that's where I recommend they start. From there, I help them assess their roles and key processes to see if they are aligned to the overarching pieces. If all of that's in place, sometimes they don't know how to manage conflict or communicate well, especially if they're stuck in the Storming phase. In the end, any team will work best if they have trust and smooth processes. To get there, we help diagnose where they are deficient against best practices, and then we help build those competencies."

"I totally get what you're describing, Orlando. It's so smart. And in ways, comforting. I like the story it tells of the way many in OD think about this work."

Orlando smiles. "Is this where we disagree?"

"After all these years, I've come to rely on a different set of assumptions about this work, so my interactions are now shaped a bit differently. I think we end up doing a lot of the same work, you and I, but perhaps it's rooted in different starting points, and those lead to different approaches and tools. Nonetheless, we'll be able to find intriguing ways to combine our practices in real time with this client."

"OK, let me have it. Both barrels." Orlando crosses his legs and folds his hand.

"Nah, there aren't any guns involved," Ava laughs. "More than anything, it's an open exploration of stories, of finding pragmatic utility, not prediction and validity. Bear with me. In my experience each team member is radically unique: gender, age, genetics, cultural heritage, education, social and economic origins, MBTI type, motivation, strengths, weaknesses, aspiration, foibles, mental illness. The list goes on.

"By definition, that makes any aggregation of individuals likewise unique. If you take any team of ten individuals and multiplied it by twenty characteristics, you begin to see what a wonderful mosaic each team is. Even if teams look similar, a team of nine salespeople might share some characteristics with other teams of nine salespeople, but in every single case, they're different.

"For every team that's unique in composition, each is also unique in its context or setting. There's literally an infinite number of settings for sales teams, from small nonprofits to Fortune 500 giants. There are organizations growing wildly or perhaps downsizing. They're in industries shaped by various pressures. They're all in some constantly emerging mix of complexity, of patterns or forces they may or may not understand or even be aware of.

"Beyond that, each unique individual gives meaning to events. They create their own narrative about what they've experienced in the past, what they're experiencing now, and what they hope to experience. Each person's story is socially constructed by the forces around them at the time. Two people from very similar circumstances will likely make vastly different stories of meaning from their experiences."

"I don't disagree," replies Orlando. "Nothing you've said is all that controversial, especially the postmodern stuff and the complexity theory underpinnings."

"Fair enough," says Ava. "Here's where the implications of all this lead me in my practice. First, I don't think we can compare this team to any other. That includes data sets about other teams, or all the teams we think might be like this one particular team. The more I sit with teams, the less valuable it seems to compare against ideal type models and best practices. Second, this then shapes the assessment we help the team engage in. If comparison is useless, then normative data doesn't help much. The question becomes: what data and data gathering process provide the most utility possible without comparison? Third, it means that each team is a unique organism worthy of understanding where they are here and now, not as compared to some developmental model. It's of little value to tell them they're "in a Storming phase" or "in Stage 3" or that they have to learn how to trust before they can have conflict. Our question becomes: How can we help the team assess where it is and whether it's making progress on their own terms without using linear or predictive models?

"A few things I know we agree on. For one, people's time is scarce. They live in a state of almost fatal 'attention poverty.' I've never once in 25 years had a team say they had plenty of time to engage in our process, whatever that may be. Our job is to help them focus on the vital few drivers of their improved effectiveness, not the proscribed levers hypothesized in other models. Furthermore, the questions we help them hold are of deep importance. Those will resonate throughout our work with them. Finally, our job is to help them see that they own this thing. They are the only ones who know what's going on here. They are the only ones who can assess themselves, who can decide what's most important to work on here and now, and who can actually do the work. Their job is to adapt to seemingly non-stop changing conditions. Our job is to equip them to do just that."

Orlando leans forward. "A lot of that sounds like what Peter Block (2009) talks about in his book Community."

"Great reference, yes. Each of these implications shapes how we structure our interactions with Juliette and the team. And that leads to the biggest implication for you and me."

"Which is...what?"

"That a good way for us to approach our work together is to put on a different set of goggles, throw away the maps that give us comfort, and join the team on a voyage of discovery. Our voyage will be largely sailless and rudderless until we help the team sew their own sails and handcraft their own rudder. All of that makes things richer and more complex, and fundamentally puts us in a place of not-knowing."

Orlando measures his words carefully. "I'll be honest with you Ava. To me, that sounds like a good bit of insanity. They'll never go for it. And it's just incredibly inefficient, maybe even unethical, not to bring to the team an existing body of knowledge derived from social science research."

Ava smiles reassuringly. "That's one narrative to construct about how this will go. A different narrative might be that the team will appreciate the chance to own this voyage, and that you and I will approach all of this with a humility and deep professionalism they'll appreciate. They might discover a lot and sail quite far by themselves after we've left."

"It just feels wrong. Or maybe less right than I'm used to. Quite frankly, it's making my toes curl with anxiety."

"I don't think it's about right and wrong. I think it's about what works best when one examines one's assumptions about teams. It's about doing justice to their unique situation. My toes curl, too. I think it's a mix of anxiety and adrenaline. I'm not sure those two things ever go away. We have a lot to learn from one another. In fact, that's the only way to start a gig like this. I literally have no idea how this will go."

"Ava, are you going to say all of that to Juliette and team?"

"Sure. It's a really good way to disrupt the stasis that's likely taken root in the team. If we do so with positive energy, empathy, and vulnerability, those are all good for us to role model."

"Ava, this makes me feel like a beginner. I don't like that feeling."

"That makes two of us. Now, let's go see Tom, and as we walk, let me share with you some of the key points from yesterday's conversation with Juliette," says Ava, and with a small smile, "and Romeo 17."

SIX

Approaching the Gatekeeper

"I call them 'Barnacles' and 'Scrapers,'" Tom says.

After settling in 10 minutes late into their 45-minute lunch meeting—running from back-to-backs between buildings, a quick reply to a text about an afternoon call, taking a sip of his third coffee of the morning—Tom, the team's Program Manager, marginally relaxes into his first conversation with Ava and Orlando.

"Oh, do the Scrapers somehow scrape the Barnacles?" asks Ava. "Is it an adversarial relationship? Or a symbiotic relationship?"

"No, not at all. In fact, they don't interact all that much. I just call them that because it captures how the two groups interact and connect inside Juliette's team. And I would never call them that to their faces. It's just my shorthand."

"Got it. I'm curious: how do the two groups work and connect?"

"The three Barnacles have been with Juliette for a few years, and they're very tightly connected to her. It's a deep relationship. They rely on her for important information about what's going on in the organization. There's deep connection and a lot of trust. And she relies on them. Their survival during these times of reorg seems more assured the more tightly they stay connected to her."

"Right. And the Scrapers?" asks Orlando.

"I call them that because the three of them are new to the team after the reorg smashed us all together. They're not deeply connected to Juliette, the Barnacles, or anything else, other than their incredibly intense workload and clients. When they're interacting with the team, they scrape the important stuff off the table and then cut and run. They have zero tolerance for fluff or anything that doesn't make their lives less crazy. Their busyness sucks all the oxygen out of the room. And it means that the small things Juliette has done to try to build some relationships, such as all going out for drinks together on Friday afternoon, hasn't made much of an impact."

"So, when all nine team members are together with Juliette, what's the vibe?," Ava probes. "How does the team use its time together?"

"Probably like you'd expect. I prepare an agenda, and for the most part I keep us tightly focused on it. But if it's not a topic of interest, people get on their phone or laptop to try to catch up with email."

"If I came and watched a meeting, what would I see?"

"Some mix of boredom, information sharing, decisions being made, a little conflict, and the occasional, if not obligatory, collaboration. We're probably more surviving than thriving. But I'm not even sure what thriving would look like here."

Tom picks through his disappointing salad and looks at his watch. "Let me ask you two a question. I pretty jealously guard this team's time. Not a single one of us has time for consultant bullshit. Whatever it is you're going to take us through is going to chew up time. The work tasks we don't get done in those hours become catch-up work in the evening. Work we'll have to do rather than play with our kids before bedtime. So, will every minute in these upcoming sessions be as valuable as every minute I would rather spend reading Goodnight Moon to my four-year-old snuggled in her fresh pajamas? Don't get me wrong. I also want to see the expected ROI for this work and the proposed timeline, and all the other things a competent PM would ask for, and I'm sure you two will win me over there. But for us nine team members, will you meet the Goodnight Moon value threshold?

"That's a challenge for all 11 of us to meet together." Ava says. "This is our time. How we use it together reflects what we all believe will bring the most value. That will demand that we together set a development agenda that makes amazing use of each rare hour we have together. I appreciate that challenge, Tom. Let's meet it together."

Reflection

As Ava and Orlando enter this particular small social ecosystem, they're confronted with narratives that convey a jumbled mix of aspiration, anxiety, challenge, and constraint. It's as if they're opening an old book and not only seeing typeface on a page, reading the text, and beginning to understand the plot, but also taking in the feel of the paper and the smell of the binding. It takes a full set of sensory, cognitive, and emotional experiences to absorb this information.

It's like trying to find the outer pieces of the jigsaw puzzle: The first step is to set boundaries and expectations both for the puzzle-solver and for the puzzle itself, if you will. Ava and Orlando surface some important assumptions and examine them for impact, understanding the way in which their assumptions will shape their earliest interactions with the client.

And that's a pretty good start.

PART THREE

Discovery

What you see and what you hear depends a great deal on where you are standing.

It also depends on what sort of person you are.

—C. S. Lewis, *The Magician's Nephew* (1955)

The activities so far set the stage for the next phase: Discovery. But this isn't OD-centric discovery, at least not at its core. It's about the *team's* process of discovery that sets the stage for their eventual decision making and action as it pertains to their quest for greater adaptability and effectiveness.

Ava and Orlando are entering the team's "river" with a single step, respecting the past, present, and future as a continuum, with a heart of hope that the team's experience is somehow better with and after them, than it has been before. They've had their first two client conversations with Juliette and Tom, and they've demonstrated curiosity, empathy, humility, and a bias for support, whatever form that may take.

Now it's time to take on the *whole.*

SEVEN

Leaving the Familiar Behind

Juliette moves a pile of yellowed flip chart papers off the remaining empty chair and takes a seat. The room still has the faint odor of lunchtime pepperoni. Ugh, she thinks. These conference rooms need a good spring cleaning. That white board has been ghosted gray with marker smudge for years...this doesn't bring me joy.

"Thanks for clearing your calendars for this short meeting. It's important that we chat together for 30 minutes or so about this new effort we're beginning to help us improve as a team. I wanted to give this specific topic our full attention rather than squeeze it into a regular staff meeting. I'm going to let Ava and Orlando introduce themselves and take over the conversation. Oh, and Ava, I hate to say it, but we have one of our members out sick with and another stuck in an airport, so we are as well-attended as we will get today. Seven out of nine isn't bad for this group."

Ava opens. "No doubt. It's a complex world, and I imagine it's rare if everyone is able to get in one room together. We will move forward, but at the end, we will need to address how those two members get up to speed on this project. Fair warning: Orlando and I are going to ask you, or some sub-set of you, to do that. So, make sure you ask all your questions."

Orlando continues. "Juliette has asked that Ava and I coach the team over the next few months on how you all can best find your way to enhanced effectiveness together. The purpose of today is to set context for that, answer your questions, and dive into the project."

"I hate to be the nay-sayer right off the bat..." says Chris.

"No, you don't," interrupts Kelly. "You actually enjoy it a bit too much."

Chris ignores Kelly. "But why would the team work on its effectiveness without Juliette?"

"Good question," says Orlando. "When we say 'the team,' we mean the 'team and leader' as an intact unit. Juliette is one member of the team, certainly in a special role. But our work together will focus on the singular and unique set of interactions of all nine people. All of that includes Juliette. And yes, to some degree, our focus at times might not include her, as you all have interactions with one another far beyond what she impacts or is even aware of."

Kelly decides to take her turn. To her, this concept of investing even more time into this team needs to be challenged up front, and frankly, defeated, if she is ever to hit her long list of deliverables. "If we're honest with ourselves, this 'team' is nothing more than the collected sticks and boxes connected under Juliette. I'm not sure there's anything super compelling about it, be it a mission, a vision, even an esprit de corps, anything, that can or should pull us together. And if there isn't, then why are we doing this?"

Ava takes this one. "There may not be, at least not yet. I'm not sure you've all even had a fair chance to have that conversation, or if such a unifying construct would be useful. I'd be curious to know if you feel like you all know each other well enough to even have a conversation like that. The question in this work will come down to something like this: What capabilities must this team have collectively—be it collaboration, communication, conflict resolution, or any number of things—so that you have the attributes and skills sufficient to deliver on what your organization, clients, and value chains demand?"

"You're going to have to give me some examples. I don't even know what that means," says Kelly.

"Sure," says Orlando. "Let's take just one aspect of teamwork, like having clear responsibilities. We'll be curious to hear if you all think they're sufficiently clear so that you can take effective action without stepping all over one another or missing important things. Or trust, for example. We have no idea how much of it you actually need in order to be able to collaborate. Is there a gap there? Only you all know the answers to those kinds of questions. And if you need those or other things, we'll help you build them."

Chris joins the challenge. "I think with all the reorgs going on around here, we'll never have trust. The folks in the executive suites get paid to dream these changes up."

"I get it," says Ava. "It's a complex world, and that never seems to let up. What we'll do in this work is only focus on this team, the people in the room. We're the only ones we can control anyway. How we respond to those constantly shifting external conditions is 100% within our control. Orlando and I will help nudge your focus back to yourselves…the nine of you."

Juliette has heard enough of the challenge, as valuable minutes have already ticked by. "I think in the last 17 minutes we should cover the project plan and discovery process. Ava, would you move us forward?"

Ava describes how the team can plan on working on the topic of improving team effectiveness over 4–6 months in an episodic way. There will be significant, more in-depth four-hour learning labs and shorter 60-minute check-in meetings. Having the team do the work together will be paramount. Success can be measured by the team's own evaluation of its ability to see, name, own, and work on the most important drivers of its effectiveness, however those are prioritized by the team.

"Finally, in the discovery interviews that start next week, Orlando and I will be asking you a series of questions about how you view the team, how its strengths and weaknesses show up in collaborative efforts, and what your deeper hopes might be for your experience on the team. We'll take a lot of notes. All of your comments will be anonymous. But when we get back together at our first learning lab in three weeks, you all will see how everyone answered the same questions, although there will be no attribution of the data to any single person. We'll then help you all find the deepest insights you can in the shortest time possible, and then those insights will guide how the team shapes its priorities for the work to come."

Silence.

"I've never been on a team where we did anything quite like that," says Dmitri. "Are you going to tell us where we're messing up and what we can do to fix it?"

"We're going to help you experience a process in which the team mines its own incredible wisdom for new ways to be effective together…to make sense, align, and create outcomes. The only real factor that will dictate how fast you get there is the courage you individually bring to the process. If you bring your story, your aspirations, your insights, then this time is likely going to fly by in a good way. I know you have more questions, and you're free to send them in an email. I also think things will become a lot clearer as we get into the work. You might just need to trust us for a little while. Our commitment to you is to never waste your time. Everything we ever do will be relevant to the life and effectiveness of this team. Here and now."

"Oh, Juliette. What in the world have you gotten us into?" says Scott, arms folded and legs crossed.

Juliette smiles. "Good stuff, I think. I hope."

EIGHT

Priming the Pump

"You're going to have to help me here, Ava." Orlando takes a seat next to her in the noisy cafe. He seems anxious, but more relaxed than in their earlier interactions.

"Sure," she says. "We've both got great tool boxes filled with relevant stuff. The two questions you'll find me asking a lot right now are: Does this particular tool help the team members express what they each find to be true and important about the team's current level of effectiveness? And does it do so in a way that honors their truly unique and complex situation without putting them in the false boundaries of normative data and predictive models?"

Orlando sips his coffee. "I'm all in. Unlock that tool box of yours and show me how this discovery interview phase goes."

"OK. I propose we put all the standard stuff at the beginning: introductions, purpose, confidentiality and anonymity, and how we and the team will use the data. Then, let's get them engaged in telling us their story, especially how they found their way into this team and what their role is. I like to ask, 'What value do you bring to the team that you think everyone is aware of, and what value do you bring that you think is largely invisible to others?' It usually sets the tone of going for deeper insights."

"I like it. Sounds clear. I assume we allow 15–20 minutes for all that?"

"Sure. Then we'll transition the interview to the more explorative questions about their perceptions of the team's effectiveness. We'll start at the broadest question and then work our way to the more specific parts. There are three major pieces to our discovery. First, take a look at these two continua." Ava opens her laptop.

Diagram 2: Interdependence and Collaboration Scales: Interview Questions.

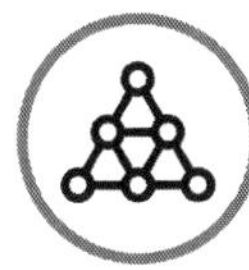

QUESTION 1.
What is this team's current state of "Interdependence," or how much team members *must depend on one another* to complete the team's work and achieve its desired outcomes?

QUESTION 2.
What is this team's current state of "Collaboration," or the degree to which team members *behaviorally demonstrate* that they can bring that interdependence to life?

"After asking the interviewee to scan the slide, we simply ask them where they would assess this team. How much interdependence does the universe demand of this team for it to be successful? And how much collaboration are they currently experiencing. They can mark anywhere low to high.

Orlando nods. "Hmm. So, what we're doing is asking them individually to assess how much interdependence is required across the team, and how much collaboration is currently evidenced that brings that interdependence to life. Are we going to average their answers? Can't we have a more precise scale, something with a firm '0' and precise gradations?"

"I'm not sure increased scalar precision is helpful. We're trying to help them tell their story, not collect precise diagnostic data. As far as averaging, I'd like to put all of their answers on the continuum and show them where the 'average' likely sits."

Orlando contemplates this. "And if there's a gap between how much interdependence is required for the team to be successful and how much collaboration is needed to get the team's work done?"

"I think that would be the team's signal to itself that collectively there's a shared belief that there's an important gap worth closing. It signals a need for important team development work not because Juliette thinks so, and certainly not because we think so, but because the team thinks so."

"Can we take all the data from the other teams you've worked with over the years and show the team what the average size gap is? Maybe help them feel less evaluated?"

"That would be normative data that compares this team to others. I don't think that's useful, as this team is unique in its composition and context. It would likely be distracting, getting their minds outside the room. So, no. We don't want to do that."

"Got it. OK, What's part two of the interview protocol?"

"See this pen I'm using? We're going to call it a magic wand, and we're going to let them use it to describe three wishes. We'll ask these three questions in order."

1. What do you imagine Juliette wants more of, less of, or that's different from the team in order to improve its effectiveness?
2. What do you imagine the entire team wants more of, less of, or that's different from Juliette in order to improve its effectiveness?
3. Taking Juliette out of it: What do you personally wish for more of, less of, or that's different from the team in order to improve its effectiveness?

"Hmm," says Orlando. "What does all this wishful thinking accomplish?"

"Primarily it makes it super simple for each person to share the narrative they've constructed about the team, in particular where there might be key gaps or tension points with the leader, but also where the individual just wishes for something else."

"What if everyone sees things differently?"

"No doubt they will, as people always see things differently. But again, we're going to trust the team's wisdom to identify the most important themes in the qualitative data."

"Can we do some factor analysis or a word cloud that distills the data for them?"

"Let's just let them read it with their own eyes. I trust that they'll make good sense of these inputs."

"Right. OK, what's the last major part of the interview protocol?"

"We're going to help each person describe what they think are the most important aspects of the team's effectiveness to work on first. What we're doing is bringing them down this funnel of inquiry to the most granular level. Take a look at this list of eight aspects of team effectiveness."

1. Psychological safety
2. Trust

3. Clear responsibilities
4. Conflict resolution
5. Clear purpose
6. Decision making
7. Norms
8. Mutual accountability

Orlando scans the slide. "It actually seems pretty standard[1]. Eight is a lot, but it covers many of the variables you see in research literature on team effectiveness."

"Great. Now we're going to ask each person two questions. 'First, where is your eye drawn to when you think about the most important lever for improving the team's effectiveness as quickly as possible—either make a strength even stronger or maybe fill some gap or fix a weakness? Pick just one...your big bet.' After they've picked one, we ask, 'OK, which one or two other elements on this sheet would most likely fuel improvement in that one key element?'"

"Let me see if I'm following. Let's say I picked accountability as the most important thing. That's what I believe would unlock our next level of effectiveness. I could then also pick two others that would help us get better at accountability, or at least help move the whole effort forward. I'd pick clear responsibilities and trust. If we had those things, then improving our accountability to one another would be easier, and that would improve our overall effectiveness. Is that the way it works?"

"Perfect. That's it."

"What if everyone picks different things? I feel like we'll be awash in slippery narratives rather than data that actually provide insights."

"They might. In fact, they're likely to. No matter what they pick, it's going to be their unique self-assessment. When we put all the responses together, it will be their puzzle to solve. It's been my experience that there will be patterns in the data, and even if they're rough patterns, they'll be insightful. We're going to trust the team's inquiry and meaning-making skills to assess what's really going on here. And that's where we earn our keep: by helping them find their own signal from the noise.

"From a Dialogic mindset, I think of this type of data as a 'sheep in wolf's clothing.' We've helped them discover their own definitions, measures, scales, and model of effectiveness. But we've done so in

---

1 This list is intended for illustration only. Any list of team characteristics or definitions can be used in Dialogic process.

a way that maintains some of their familiarity with data itself. People tend to get some comfort in data. We've given them a toehold into their most insightful conversation without bringing in outside distractions. And we've done it quickly, as there is no time and attention for endless orating. We've helped them take responsibility for sharing their narrative in succinct ways."

Orlando feels cautious. "Wow. That's a lot to cover in 55 minutes."

"If we do it effectively, their thinking will be deep, their answers will be relatively short, and the insights will be profound. Or at least intriguing. It's fun to help them convert the story in their head into actual spoken words."

"And I bet they'll be fascinated to hear what their colleagues' answers are," adds Orlando.

"Exactly," says Ava. "We've primed the pump for transparency and authenticity. We'll create a safe container for the conversation. And their curiosity will help everyone share and make meaning from the data without any of our external diagnosis, normative benchmarks, or models. The narrative is theirs to read and write. The meaning is theirs to make. The complexity is theirs to parse. And we begin to discover with them some incredibly impactful ways we can help."

NINE

Feeling the Fog but Seeing the Light

With all interviews complete, Ava and Orlando meet with Juliette to review the data and prepare for the upcoming team meeting.

"I'm glad you sent a pre-read of the data yesterday. I really needed last night and this morning to soak on it. It's so…" Juliette's voice trails off as she closes her office door. Orlando and Ava settle in.

"So…?" prompts Orlando.

"Clear. Relieving. Concerning. Befuddling. Intriguing. I have a whole mix of reactions when reading and re-reading it. Is this the kind of data you usually get on a team? It makes us seem so abnormal. And it makes me feel so not up to the task."

Ava nods. "All very natural reactions. I don't want to spend our scarce time comparing this team to others, Juliette. Let's leave the comparison here: every team is radically unique, but also very much the same. Humans are humans, and they're generally seeking the same things. Our task today is to take a look at the three unique data sets of this team, see what meaning you make of them, and then prep for our first learning lab with the team next Monday. Sound good?"

"Sure. Let's do this."

Orlando puts the first two printouts on the table. "What do you see in this interdependence and collaboration data, Juliette?"

"A few things jump right out at me. First, there's a substantial gap between what people think is the interdependence required of us and the collaboration we're currently showing. I guess it's good to know they sense that too. Second, there are almost two groups of data. Two clusters of answers. It makes me wonder if there's some reality of having two previously separated sub-teams joined together in the last reorg. Finally, there are a few outliers, with answers both really

Diagram 3: Interdependence and Collaboration Scales: Interview Answers.

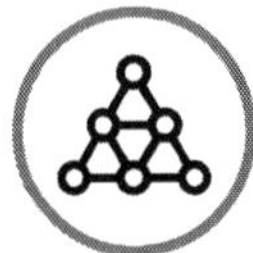

QUESTION 1.
What is this team's current state of "Interdependence," or how much team members *must depend on one another* to complete the team's work and achieve its desired outcomes?

QUESTION 2.
What is this team's current state of "Collaboration," or the degree to which team members *behaviorally demonstrate* that they can bring that interdependence to life?

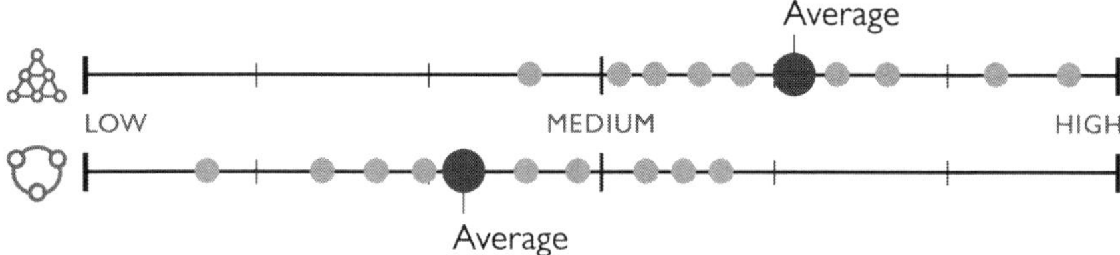

high and really low on the scale. I'm curious who those people are. Can you share with me who they are?"

Orlando answers quickly. "Our promise of anonymity to the participants means that we can't tell you who they are. But next Monday, the whole team is going to review this data, and people will have a chance to identify where they put their votes."

"One idea we can discuss later," adds Ava, "is that it might prime the pump a bit for the team's self-disclosure if you share with the team where you put your own answers on these questions. But back to your observations. Yes, the distribution of votes and clusters may indicate what you infer they do. It will be fascinating to see if the team connects the dots the same way. There might be some logic as you describe, or maybe some other pattern to the clusters, or maybe no pattern at all. The team will need to be their own social scientists."

Ava leans back and lets Orlando lead again. I like his confidence to carry these messages. I'm looking forward to debriefing this with him.

Orlando continues. "How about this second data set? The one with the three magic wand sets of answers?"

Table 3: Summaries of Answers to Magic Wand questions.

SUMMARIES OF "WHAT I IMAGINE IS..."

JULIETTE'S WISH OF THE LT	THE LT'S WISH OF JULIETTE	THE LT'S WISH OF EACH OTHER
1. Get to know one another 2. Act like a committed team 3. Embrace diversity and inclusion 4. Act respectfully 5. Do more without me 6. Be role models for great leadership to your teams	1. Help us understand why we're here in this team 2. Provide more focus and help with prioritization (saying "no" or taking things off the list) 3. Mediate our conflicts about responsibilities	1. Share your strategy so that we can get aligned 2. Do things to build trust 3. Provide support/ caring; celebrate wins together 4. Seek a balance between individual and team goals

"Wow. There's so much here. I'm 100% relieved that they can describe what I've been saying I want more of from them. I guess some of my explicit and implicit messaging about how I'd like them to communicate more is getting through. It might not be showing up in behaviors yet, but at least they're aware of it. Regarding what they want from me: some of that is a shock, some of it I totally get, and some of it they will never get from me. If they want some of those things, they'll have to get it from one another or do without."

Ava leans in. "Can you give us an example?"

Juliette leans back, folding her arms, a steely gaze in her eyes. "A few of the comments suggest they want me to set all of their priorities for them. These people are well-paid directors who should be fully capable of setting their own priorities, especially if they'd just talk with one another rather than put me at the hub of everything. I'd appreciate it if they'd grow up and stop asking me to be some omniscient parent."

"I hear your frustration," Ava gently offers. "One way to read these comments is that the reorg has shifted so many things simultaneously, they don't know where to turn for something clarifying. It's going to be helpful if some of the people can give context to their needs stated here."

Orlando adds, "I think we have some really good tools to help them have a great conversation about these topics. I want to encourage you to hold your frustration or defensiveness gently. Stay really curious about where each person is coming from, what makes sense in their experience. Listen deeply to what's being said and not said. I think there's a ton for everyone to learn in this section. Let us lead the dialogue."

Juliette pauses. "Is this..."

"If you want to know if this is 'normal,' I'm willing to say, 'yes,'" answers Ava. "Many leaders read this section and end up feeling blind-sided or attacked or frustrated. There are limits to your own narrative about this team. None of your team members know the story you tell yourself about this team, just as you don't know theirs. You're not omniscient. In no scenario could you ever be. Nor could Orlando and I. But what will help the team in the upcoming meeting is for you to be balanced and curious about what they think and feel. Ask good questions."

"Fair enough. But if in the moment you see me getting too amped up or too defensive, can you call a break and help me recalibrate?"

"Sure. And you can too. Let's partner on helping you and the team have the most insightful conversation possible, even if we wade into unexpected places. Quickly, let's look at the last data set."

Orlando pulls out the last slides. "What do you see here, Juliette?"

Table 4: Summaries of Answers to Drivers of Improved Effectiveness Question.

Primary Improvement	Secondary	Secondary
Clear Purpose	Norms	Trust
Clear Responsibilities	Clear Purpose	Norms
Clear Purpose	Psychological Safety	Decision Making
Norms	Conflict Resolution	Clear Purpose
Clear Purpose	Clear Responsibilities	Trust
Trust	Norms	Mutual Accountability
Trust	Clear Purpose	Norms
Clear Purpose	Norms	Mutual Accountability
Decision Making	Trust	Norms

"I actually see remarkable alignment. We don't all see the same priorities, but we have a lot of the same focus areas. This actually helps me feel highly encouraged. Are you two going to present this as our development agenda for the next few months?"

Orlando pauses, deferring to Ava. "We're going to help the team tap into its own discernment and mine its wisdom. The dialogue process we run will help the team get to alignment on what we'll call a hypothesis or a generative image. The team and you must take an act of ownership by putting your limited time and attention on just a few key elements. We can't do that for you. We're here to support any bet the team wants to make. It will be some statement of intent and possibility that's shaped by this first process of inquiry.

"Here's the kicker. We won't end this meeting without one. So, if Orlando and I can't facilitate the team to some apt conclusion, we will defer to you to select a concrete focus area based on all the data and dialogue the team will have had. You and the team must own this statement together. But pragmatism will rule the day. We will move forward from next Monday's meeting with a really clear stimulus for the hard work that unfolds over the next few months."

Juliette hops up from her chair. "Oh no. This meeting's gone 15 minutes longer than I have scheduled." She is late for her next meeting with her EVP. Putting on her coat, she pauses, looking at Ava and Orlando directly.

"Thank you. Both. This was incredibly illuminating. I have no idea where this is all going, but I trust you're going to help us get somewhere positive and important. Do you really think the team is ready to step up and own this together?"

"I literally have no idea," says Ava. "But your team members treated the interview as an important step. They seem invested. Many wouldn't stop talking. And they seem to want something different. We'll take it all one step at a time. Something will emerge, and we're as intrigued as you are to see where all this goes."

Reflection

Orlando and Ava accomplish most of what they want to in the discovery process. They begin the process of having each diverse voice be heard as they assemble the major components of each person's story about the team. They start to learn the language of the team, the metaphors they use, and the suspicions that ride in the back of their minds. They validate each person's experience as they prepare the team to engage in focusing and decision making about its development agenda.

They also signal to the client that quick diagnosis and canned solutions won't be part of the way the project unfolds. Rather, they'll be helping the client see and name things in an emerging, rich narrative, and that in so doing, a stage will be set for the team's ownership of the work ahead.

In their focused, pragmatic approach, they include self-imposed limits. They need to see both the forest and trees, and in so doing, cut corners. They clearly do not have time to inventory the full complexity or the deep narrative of all viewpoints. They compromise when it comes to sharing with Juliette each insight they had developed through the interviews. They bring focus and prioritization to their debrief with Juliette, and still the meeting goes long.

In short: They create minimum sufficient contextualization for the work to be able to continue. Their inquiry is itself an intervention, although it doesn't feel that way to anyone. It is curious, balanced, and pragmatic. It avoids measures and models that begin to box the team in. It is masterful use of a trowel, not a scalpel.

That's a lot for one week.

PART FOUR

Mining, Focusing, and Owning

Always remember: Your focus determines your reality. —Master Yoda[2]

Be careful not to choke on your aspirations. —Darth Vader[3]

Honoring generativity, complexity, and narrative (Bushe & Marshak, 2015), we relieve ourselves of the burden of concepts of eternal rights and wrongs, *musts* and *shoulds*, good and evil. Each narrative is touched with some mix of hero and villain, saint and sinner, light and dark, context and character, pathos, ethos, and logos. Both Yoda and Vader have things to teach us; the emergence of one character shapes the definition of the other.

For the team to move forward in this work in a productive and pragmatic way, they require a healthy container. One might think of this container as the necessary time, space, and process within which meaning can be made or found in their multi-faceted stories. That process is internal to the team, not one imposed from diagnostic models outside the team. They themselves form the container for the work now manifest, their narratives reside within, and we help hold and attend to that container for and with them.

For Ava and Orlando, their skill must lie in helping the team mine for insights, judiciously focus, and claim ownership of their development. Knowing that the team members may not be fully or equally equipped for that work yet, they can encourage them to muster the courage to take all steps possible on the journey.

A crystalizing question, perhaps a clear if-then hypothesis, is an important way to help a team claim ownership. An intriguing generative image (Bushe, 2020) that sucks in old problems and spins off new possibilities can also help a team connect to something bigger than the current sum of their parts.

2 From *Star Wars, Episode I: The Phantom Menace* (Lucas, 1999).

3 From *Rogue One: A Star Wars Story* (Emanuel, Kennedy, Shearmur, & Edwards, 2016).

TEN

Plan/No Plan

"What's the goal here, Ava? What's the bottom line of our upcoming time with Juliette and team?" Orlando's other client work has taken him to another time zone for three days, and a video call will have to suffice for preparing for the upcoming learning lab meeting. A poor Wi-Fi connection and this call are all that stand between him and some hard-earned room service food.

Ava begins. "I think about this in three ways. First, we'll help the team share their perspectives about what came out of the discovery interviews. I have no idea what they'll make of it, and we should be prepared to have new data enter the conversation. Second, we'll help them discern the trivial from the important. There's too much to attend to, so we have to help them focus by finding out what's a bit more trivial, and then stripping that away. They need to be miners for insights. They need tunnel vision. Think of it as a refiner's fire in a crucible. What's left when everything has burned off? The precious material.

"Third, we're going to help them SNOW: See, Name, Own, and Work. The first two things I mentioned are part of Seeing and Naming, but we need to help them Own a choice about their first focus area in their development journey. Whatever that is, whatever will help them close their current interdependence–collaboration gap will direct us as we help them Work on it."

"Got it. I imagine it will be important for us to facilitate in a way that slows down when that seems right, speeds up when that's right, and builds some sense of psychological safety so that they can trust and be open with one another, right?"

"Exactly. Help the unsaid become said, help the invisible emerge, even if at times that scares them. Fear and anxiety are almost always a part of this work. Theirs and ours. By the way, can you draft a loose agenda with topics but almost no timeframes? If they don't have an agenda, they'll be like squirrels looking for nuts on a frosty Autumn morning. We'll help them feel comfortable enough about the mundane so that we can help them get uncomfortable about the profound."

"I'm on it. I have a nagging fear that there are ways you and I might get lost in the room if we don't have a really well-rehearsed plan. But I'll catch up with you early next week for final prep, and we can talk it through then."

"Safe travels, Orlando. This is going to be great."

ELEVEN

Deciphering and Making Meaning

Ava and Orlando arrive at the conference room early. Seated at the far end is Craig, arms crossed, staring intently at his laptop as if it had said something simultaneously confusing and insulting to him. Craig had sat in that particular chair for the better part of five years, tracking budget, approving spend, and giving Juliette financial insights free of any entanglements that would cause her confusion or grief. He glances up at the disturbance and recognizes Orlando and Ava from the kick-off meeting and interview.

"I don't do team building. Can't stand it. I'm here early only because I need to get a report out before this thing starts." Craig's knee bounces under the table nonstop, a bass drum playing to some anxiety-fueled anthem only he can hear.

"That makes three of us," says Orlando, taking time to circle over to Craig, look him in the eye, and shake his hand. "We can't stand it either, at least as it's usually done. Don't worry. No trust falls, OK? We'll try to stay quiet as we set up so you can focus for a while."

Juliette and Chris enter 10 minutes later, deep in conversation about next quarter's marketing push. Juliette holds her hand up to Chris, pausing the conversation, and looks at Ava. "Can't believe it, but we'll be two short today. Jeff is home with a sick baby, and Aisha has a critical client meeting for the next hour. She'll join when she's done there. Otherwise, we should have everyone." Without waiting for a reply, she returns her focus to Chris.

Ava and Orlando's eyes meet, eyebrows arched, small, pained smiles hidden from the rest. It always goes this way. "Whoever shows up are the right people," whispers Ava, squaring up a stack of Post-It Note pads that need no discernible squaring.

Tom strides in, glancing at the clock. "Let's go, people. Time is money, and time's a wasting. Ready, Ava?"

As Ava and Orlando guide the team through the first visual data set that shows the perceived gap between interdependence and collaboration, people pretty freely tell each other where they had placed their votes. That transparency is quickly followed by rhetorical questions about how others could possibly think that was the way it was.

The insight, however, is cemented by Dmitri. "I don't know if it matters too much if any single one of us is right. I think the big picture matters most: we have a gap. Our current collaboration isn't sufficient to get us where we need to go. I hear what every one of us is saying, but I want to see if we can hear what everyone is saying. Altogether. We have work on us to do."

You never know where it's going to come from, but it seems like it's often the quiet ones that bring the most wisdom, muses Ava.

The second data set, the one with the three magic wand summaries, lands with a thud. Juliette can barely contain her frustration at what she perceives everyone is demanding of her. This kind of feedback triggers her subtle perfectionism. While the Barnacles know it, and had known it for some time now, the Scrapers are just learning it: for Juliette, frustration can quickly blossom into righteous indignation.

The story is being written as we speak, notices Orlando. This moment...this IS the story. We're talking about it and writing it simultaneously. How weird is that?

The data, nonetheless, is really helpful for the team to begin an exploration of what they most deeply want from one another, once they take Juliette and her strong reaction out of the mix.

The third data set, which holds everyone's beliefs about the key drivers of the team's future improved effectiveness, initially signals to the team something unprofessionally prepared. Ava wants to trust the team's ability to make sense of the data, but with its lack of pre-sorting and sifting, it comes across as poorly done.

Chris smells blood in the water first. "I really think these data should be in a pivot table."

"Yeah, it would make it easier for us to grasp what you're trying to tell us and understand how you'll direct our development," joins Kelly.

Orlando fills the space. "It matters less how we present it, and it doesn't matter at all what Ava and I make of it. The only thing that matters is what you make of it. What do you see when you look at it? What is the team saying to one another about what it needs most right now? About what it aspires to? About the living, breathing 'puzzle' this team needs to get solved?"

Ava helps move the conversation forward. "I want you to take two minutes silently by yourself, to look at this data set. If you were forced to discern what the biggest drivers of this team's future collaboration might be, what would you highlight? After that, I want you to huddle with two teammates, and as a threesome create some shared view, even if you agree only 75% or so. And then, we'll take a lunch break. When we come back, we'll hear your reports as a large group."

"I don't know if I'm up for this," says Scott, leaning back in his chair, arms folded.

"No worries," says Orlando. "Simply listening is a perfectly fine form of active participation. Is that something you're able to do over the next few minutes?"

"I'll give it a try."

TWELVE

A Quiet Statement of Focus and Ownership

After lunch, Ava brings the team's focus to the flip chart papers illustrating each sub-team's report out. "Team One, can we hear your voice? Can one of you read your statement to the team?"

Dmitri stands and explains their thought process, concluding with, "We have to get clear on why this team exists and settle on some healthy behavioral norms."

"Thanks. Team Two. You're next."

Aisha, who had returned from her urgent client meeting during the lunch break, reads their point of view. "We want to trust each other more. If we do, all sorts of things will get better."

"Great, thanks. And team Three?"

Kelly navigates her wheelchair to the front of the room, weaving her way through the jumble of chairs. "This may be unpopular, but we still think Juliette needs to do more to help us get really clear on why these people are on this team, who does what, and then play a more active role in helping manage the conflict we have."

"OK. Thank you all for that work. Now...what do you make of all three of these points of view together? What are you saying to one another?"

Tom goes first. "Listening to Team 3, I disagree, and I'm not sure it's on Juliette to do all that. If we are truly going to Own and Work on this together as a team, then I think we have to take that on together. I also agree with Team 1. I'd say an important part of our work together is to decide why we are here, especially post-reorg. We owe it to ourselves to be 100% clear on our purpose. Full stop. My hunch is that some of the conflict would simply go away if we got that figured out."

"I'd like to share my perspective with the trust part of #2," offers Chris. "I don't think we don't trust each other. I just think we don't know each other yet, so trust just hasn't formed. We don't spend much time together, and when we do, agendas are packed tight. If I knew you all better, I'd trust you more. Anyway, we're already achieving so many of our goals. Think about how much better that will get if we have better relationships and clear purpose."

"Let me summarize what I've heard, because it's really important we crystallize this," says Ava. "I hear you saying that if you get to know one another better, formed some solid relationships, took some time to really explore why this team's together—its purpose—and the value you're capable of creating together, that those would be important first steps toward improving your collaboration and effectiveness. Is that right?"

Silence.

"Yes," says Juliette, who had been silent for the last 20 minutes. "I believe that's a good and true statement. I know I would feel so much better if we did those things. Even as just a first step."

"What about norms and mutual accountability? Conflict resolution? Those were all listed on that handout from our interview data," says Craig, knee still bouncing.

"What about if we do this one step at a time, taking up whatever the team feels are the right order of steps?" offers Orlando. "It might just be if we get to know and trust each other, and figure out a purpose, that healthy norms might emerge along the way. We can pick up some of these other topics from a position of growing strength and capability."

"I love this," says Aisha. "I'd like to state this another way, if that's OK. Something visual. We're a team. We are the people who are here, for whatever reason that may be. And we wish to be something more or different, whatever that will be. We're in some wonderful tension between the us of today at…," she pauses and looks at the clock "…at 1:57 p.m., and the us of tomorrow at 1:57 p.m. Or next week or next month or next year at 1:57 p.m."

Scott is suddenly done listening. He jumps up and draws a picture on the whiteboard of a clock at 1:57. "That could be just the image for everything we want and need. A picture of a clock face set to 1:57. The image itself tells us, and only us, that we're on some path to something different, no matter where we came from. This is our moment of agreement to something important, even if we don't fully know what it is. It's the big question: what do we want to be at 1:57 tomorrow? How do we close our own gap?"

Smiles. And a good silence fills the room. For a moment, the team has created a small instance of a Wonderful World.

Orlando stands to close the 4-hour working session. "Before we wrap today, we're going to do some concrete, super-simple action planning. Ava and I are going to design our next working session to focus on getting to know each other better and a way to create a purpose, as you've all decided. Now, what are 2–5 things that you can do to help move things forward until we meet again in three weeks? Just call out your ideas, and we'll make sense of them together."

The team arrives at three actions.

First, Dmitri will bring Jeff, who had missed the session due to an ill child, up to speed on the discussion and next steps.

Second, Aisha, whom Tom would think of as a Scraper, and Kelly, whom Tom would describe as a Barnacle, will have a cup of coffee to explore how the two groups might interact more. They suspect there may be common points of shared interest, information to share, maybe early warning systems. Just small things they might experiment with.

Finally, Juliette and Tom agree to think about how more time and space for conversation could be a part of their weekly meeting agendas.

Ava leaves them one more request. "Would you all spend 30 minutes with one another individually and just chat sometime before our next learning lab? Would you prioritize that? Just discover and enjoy."

Orlando and Ava walk through the parking lot. "You know what I discovered today? Sometimes, you have to profoundly not know what's going to happen in order to let happen the only thing that ever could," muses Orlando.

"Wow. That resonates," Ava replies. "I discovered sometimes, healing steals in like a rising tide. It's subtle. You can't notice it in the moment, you just start to feel it."

Reflection

Ava and Orlando help the team SNOW (see, name, own, work). They do so without taking the team's mind outside the room to other Diagnostic models, measures, or comparisons. They help the team find its own data with high degrees of utility, availability, and internal validity. Whether the team realizes it or not, they are already establishing new norms.

Ava and Orlando help them find their most important thing, a crystalizing hypothesis and a generative image (the clock at 1:57), and now the team owns it. They set the stage for the team and Juliette to move forward toward the pragmatic improvements that will increase their effectiveness, and they do so while helping the team discover new layers of vulnerability and transparency, which fosters deeper levels of trust.

That must feel pretty good.

PART FIVE

Pragmatic Improvements

I look for what needs to be done. After all, that's how the universe designs itself.

—R. Buckminster Fuller (1964)

Team coaches like Ava and Orlando often carry two overarching goals amid all this work: help seed *hope* where there may be none, and fuel *momentum* as a new reality begins to bud and blossom. This is part alchemy, part architecture, and part adaptation.

The team's new hypothesis and generative image begin to shape the planning for the upcoming learning labs. Ava and Orlando will need to hold these loosely, as the team might discover along the way that an even more important and urgent topic deserves their attention. While that can frustrate a plan-oriented coach, it's also the ultimate act of team ownership: controlling their time, prioritization, and focus in a way that creates the greatest, shared value possible.

THIRTEEN

The Salient Sea

Even as Orlando discovers his laptop battery is dead, Tom taps on the fish tank glass, and Juliette texts her EVP, Ava dives right in. "Juliette, Tom...it's great to have these 45 minutes to share how Orlando and I anticipate the team will engage in the next 4-hour meeting. We want to spend the first 30 minutes today chatting with both of you, and then for the last 15 minutes, we'd like to talk to Juliette alone to cover some stuff relating to the role of the leader in these sessions. Orlando, ready to roll?"

He introduces the biggest piece of work for the team to engage in: the team's purpose conversation. "Success will mean helping the team discover its most salient why: its purpose. What is the core reason this team exists in this complex ecosystem? The answer to that might be something the four of us think is relatively small, or it could be something that makes angels sing. Regardless, Ava and I will help the team write a story together that includes a compelling purpose. We've also left some slack in the agenda so that we can pick up another topic if something important emerges. Right now, we're prepared to help the team discover the norms, or commonly followed 'rules of the road' you all want to live by as you bring the purpose to life through action.

"The conversation will be both structured and organic, and the participants should find it really engaging to work together on these topics. Regarding getting to know one another and build trust, we're going to be doing some micro-bursts of conversation designed to help you build layers of this. These will be 15–20-minute chats that should challenge you in a good way to be transparent...even vulnerable, but in a way that builds on the existing levels of safety and trust."

"I'd like to see if we can start measuring trust," interjects Tom.

"OK. Say more," says Orlando.

"I think if it's as important as everyone says, then we should be measuring our progress over time, maybe measuring it at our team meetings, or maybe comparing our trust scores to other teams. I think seeing progress will help make it more real."

"I really like the seed of this idea, Tom," says Orlando. "I'm a huge fan of data. Ava and I enjoy helping teams collect their most important data, but we're a bit picky when it comes to introducing measures. We're not fans of comparing this team to any other. Would you be OK if you and I work offline together on this idea? Trade some emails over the next few days? I think there are some cool ways we can help you help the team find really good measures that help you track change over time, if they're also comfortable with that."

Tom agrees.

Orlando continues. "Throughout the meeting, we're going to follow the team's energy. We made a commitment to you to only work on relevant things, to meet the "Goodnight Moon" value threshold criteria. This is not a meeting where something happens to people, it's where people do something to and for themselves. It's a 'full-contact sport.'"

With Tom excused, Juliette answers Ava's first question. "It was really hard at first, just listening to the team talk and talk at the last learning lab, almost without me. Listening is hard when you're supposed to be in charge of everyone and everything." Juliette gazes out the window and then gets up and walks over to the fish tank.

Ava presses gently. "Did it get any easier over the 45 minutes? What did you experience? I was watching you, but I couldn't tell what you were thinking."

"I found myself less listening to the discussion and more just watching them and soaking it all in. Thinking about them. That changed, though, into deeply appreciating them. Don't get me wrong. I was listening to it all, and I agree with the hypothesis and image of the clock at 1:57. But I just so deeply admired the way Dmitri handled himself and helped the others. I see new potential in him I hadn't seen before. I love that Kelly maneuvered her wheelchair through the obstacle course to the front of the room, when she could have easily stayed where she was. She has so much courage and presence I never noticed underneath her abrasive tone. I liked that Scott sat there the entire time with his arms folded until he jumped up and grabbed a marker to draw the clock on the whiteboard. And to have Kelly and Aisha agree to explore touchpoints between the two groups. I was blown away. They're both so busy right now. It's all more than I thought possible. It makes me now realize they don't need me as much as I thought they did."

"The beauty here is that they're growing, but you're all in one ecosystem, growing together. Maybe all in one fish tank together." Ava smiles at Juliette and continues. "Their growth creates both change and opportunity for you. Your effectiveness is intrinsically and intimately connected to theirs. These things change together, or else they never really change. Maybe you can stop doing some things and start doing some new things. Experiment with small changes and see what happens. There are probably some new things to get really good at. Like helping them be highly effective together, here and now. We can help you discover that."

Juliette leans forward. "Is that the big point here? That the team is starting to write a new story together? I only partially get that. And I admit it feels weird to think that I'm not going to be the heroine in this tale. That's how I roll. Or have rolled. That's going to be hard to give up. I feel weird. In my gut."

"This can be simultaneously simple and complicated. It's all learning, which makes it daunting and beautiful," says Ava softly.

Juliette gazes out the window, brow furrowed. "OK, thanks. Have to run. I'm the guest tasting judge at the division's cookie, cake, and pie competition. Time to smile..."

FOURTEEN

Clarity

Juliette takes her chair and notices that the whiteboard is whiter than she has seen in years. Looking up, she sees the air ventilation ducts no longer have spider webs on them. "What's with the Spring cleaning?" she asks no one in particular.

Scott says, "I figured that if we were going to See, Name, Own, and Work this team, I'd get my friend from Facilities to repay a favor he owes me. He and I worked on the whiteboard. And we're replacing the broken chairs. Cleaned up nicely, eh?"

Juliette silently mouths thank you to him as Orlando addresses the team. "We'd like to start with a 15-minute opening conversation to get us grounded. I'd like you to pair up with someone you know less well. Please take a chair next to someone now."

As they rearrange, he pulls up a slide that has three questions. He'll show only one question at a time, and as he does, the team members will ask each other the questions, taking turns answering.

1. What do you love most in life?
2. What do you fear most in life?
3. What do you hope for most in life?

As it goes with this tool, the conversations are huddled and quietly intense. People are looking each other in the eye, listening deeply, nodding, connecting.

Orlando struggles to regain their attention amid protests for more time from Jeff and the need to do this with everyone from Kelly. "Sorry," says Orlando. "We have a lot to dig into today. But here's the great thing. You can do this with each other all the time. You now have the tool, the growing feelings of trust, and the new team norm that this is an OK thing to do with each other and for each other. Pretty cool, right? Let's move on. Ava?"

Ava stands. "Here's how we're going to explore the purpose

conversation today. The team will start by identifying their 3–4 most important stakeholder groups. Then you'll work in small subgroups aligned to a stakeholder group to identify what each needs most from this team. Focus on those things that only this team can provide. Put yourselves in that stakeholder's shoes and imagine why what we do is so critically important to them.

"In short, the purpose of this exercise is to cover the walls with flip chart paper that immerse us in the world of the people who consume what we produce, who rely on us to be very good at what we do. In short, identify the deeply important *what we do* and the difference it makes in their lives. Ready to begin?"

The team digs right in, but not without struggle. The reorg had injected some new stakeholder groups, just as it had also brought in new team members, those whom Tom called Scrapers. Getting to know one another's stakeholders, and by extension their business imperatives, was a discovery process all in itself. That took longer than Ava and Orlando expected. Not only was time flying by, it seemed to be compressing itself. Ava cuts in. "Our next step is to take those insights and ask ourselves these questions: What's this team's critical role in this broader ecosystem of stakeholders? Why are the nine of us in proximity? What joins us? What happens to this organization if we don't do what we're called to do? In short, why does this team exist?"

As the groups reconvene, Juliette breaks the silence. "I think I heard it in what Tom just said." She has been both working in a breakout group and also roaming among groups, listening in, asking probing and challenging questions. She has a focus and energy Ava and Orlando have not seen before. She picks up a marker and facilitates at the whiteboard, as Ava and Orlando sit and quietly watch. "Try this: 'This leadership team exists to create enhanced value across the division by selling and delivering existing high-quality client solutions, acting as an early sensing system for industry trends, and driving new, integrated approaches across our key stakeholder groups. We integrate those efforts as collaborative leaders in an inspiring way to create a path forward for our employees and stakeholders.' How does that sound?"

Silence. Again, that good silence.

"It's at least 80/20, if not 90/10," says Aisha. "A bit generic, but it brings in the stuff we all do. I can see myself in it, and I appreciate the client focus. Plus, there's some stretch in it, some new stuff. And, it feels like another '1:57 moment.' Like we're discovering something important on the path between what we had before we walked into this room and we're walking out with now. Something new that pushes us into the future."

"Great," says Ava. "After a break, we'll get closure on this and then move onto Norms."

Returning to their places at the table after the break, Craig approaches Ava. "Tom and I were talking, and we think we should pause on norms. In some ways, they're already starting to get clearer and better. What we need to work on is figuring out how each of us connects to the team's purpose, and further, to one another. I can't say I really know what everyone is responsible for. As the finance guy, I need to make sure we're all aligned on cost allocations, but that's pretty tactical. I just need us to get really clear on our roles."

Tom joins in as others tune into the conversation. "Agree. I need us to do what Craig is saying so I can ensure we're running our timelines aligned and efficiently."

Juliette, who has receded again, adds "I want to do both what Craig and Tom are talking about, plus I want to work on norms. Do we have time to do it all?"

Ava's kicking herself for not seeing this coming, and for reasons she can't describe, a deep anxiety is getting the best of her. She hasn't felt like this in quite some time. Orlando senses this. "Hey Ava, what would you think about a WOL?" Ava and Orlando had talked about what to do if and when they got lost, when the narratives became too complex, or when the flow of the session seemed "off." They would Whisper Out Loud, or WOL. They'd just push the pause button and let the team listen in real time as the two of them sorted out how they'd find their way back to a good path forward. (See Lipmanowicz and McCandless, 2014, for a compendium of relevant facilitative tools.)

Ava sits down. "Oh, my goodness. Yes. Let's do that. Help me think this through."

"I think I know where and why you got lost. I did too," begins Orlando. "We can debrief that later. Would it be helpful if we focus the next hour in the agenda on charters? I think Tom and Craig are right, and it seems to be what the team wants to discover next."

Ava nods. She appreciates Orlando's empathy, but she's 'lost the thread.' She needs him to bring some structured thought to what comes next. She needs to sit and watch for a while, not lead.

Table 5: Charter Template

Why does my *team* exist? It's unique purpose?

-
-
-

Who does my *team* serve?
Stakeholders? Employees? Clients?

-
-
-

What are the objectives and desired outcomes my *team* will be held accountable for? What are the key activities?

-
-
-

What are my *team's* key quantitative and qualitative measures and key results that show success?

-
-
-

What are my *team's* key interfact points?
Internal team meetings? Topics? Milestones?
Contact points outside this team?

-
-
-

"How about I pull up that charter template from my hard drive and kick us off on that work? Would that work for you, Juliette? Ava?" Hearing no objection, Orlando introduces the team to a thought process by which they can gain clarity on each person's "why, what, and how."

"Take 15 minutes individually to start filling in the most important information other people should know about the team or organization you lead. Put your answers on flip chart paper. Then we'll share these with one another in a gallery walk around the room. The point of all this is to find our most important points of connection, possible gaps, and charter conflicts. We'll do this at a high level today, and in the weeks that follow, you can continue to refine them."

After reviewing the eight sub-team charters, the four hours have flown, barely leaving Orlando enough time for the action planning process and check out conversation. He ends with a closing observation. "We've created today a first look at the things that appropriately both connect and divide you as a team. Some things connect you in value chains and join you in a common purpose rooted in your stakeholders' needs. The things that divide you are the right things. They're the things that differentiate and create clarity that help you know what's yours, his, hers, and ours. These boundaries help ensure that important things don't get muddled or missed.

"These answers may shift in the future, as you live in a complicated and complex world. But the capability being built inside the team is the ability to both get clear and then adapt the big and little things in your emergent world. You're all just humans doing your best together to pursue the things you love, to avoid the things you fear, and work toward the things you hope for."

"You know," says Tom, "this is the first time I've felt connected to something 'bigger' in this organization. The irony is, it's not to the organization itself. It's to this team. I really don't care much about the corporate values and mission as much as I care about us and this. This is worth my time."

Silence. The good kind.

Reflection

Ava and Orlando continue to help the team write its new, shared story. The team's discoveries come in the big, the small, and the connected filaments that hold them together. That newly discovered connective tissue can be hard to see, but Ava and Orlando help it become a bit more visible, likely for the first time.

They also discover more about themselves, their strengths and weaknesses, and their partnership. They find that they need one another. They each carry their own internally valid wisdom and tools, and they find powerful ways to combine them.

Pragmatism rules the day: simple and completable actions link to the desired future state, with maximum impact for minimal, efficient effort.

Not bad work, if you can get it.

PART SIX

Exit

One's destination is never a place but rather a new way of looking at things.

—Henry Miller (1957)

Over the past five months, Ava and Orlando have stepped into the team's flowing river of experience and changed it with their presence. As the time to step out of that river nears, their focus turns toward helping Juliette and Tom consolidate their learning about the team and themselves. What's been discovered in the team and in themselves as leaders? Beyond that, Ava and Orlando have also discovered themselves as a team, and as such, have their own tentative conclusions to reach.

It's time to reflect.

FIFTEEN

The Meaning Made

Something is off, thinks Ava. Did she change the lighting in here?

"Sorry this debrief meeting had to move a few times," says Juliette. "Had to fly to HQ for some impromptu strategy meetings. It's been what, four weeks, since our final learning lab session?"

Ava sets the context. "Yes, four weeks. Time flies. The purpose of this meeting is for the four of us to get closure on our five months of work together. Orlando and I want to hear about how things have changed on the team, how you experienced the support we provided, and what you hope to discover in the team looking forward. Like before, we'll spend a part of the time together, then for the last portion, Tom, we'll give you 30 minutes back while Juliette, Orlando, and I chat."

"No worries. I'll go first then," responds Tom. "So, my top line assessment is that I guess you're going to have to call me a bit of a convert." A small smile creases across his usually stoic face. "I've seen lots of changes in how the team works, even though it would be pretty hard for me to totally describe or quantify it."

"Great. Can you give us some examples?" prompts Orlando.

"Sure. Regarding the things I pay attention to, I hear quite a bit less confusion among team members. They seem to have found ways of just reaching out and solving things themselves without bringing in the PM office. As they've gotten to know one another, the walls have come down more quickly."

"Nice. What else?"

"The clear purpose we now have has calmed us down. The charters took a while to hammer out, and wow, did that process ever surface some important gaps and overlaps in our responsibilities. We hadn't fully appreciated how the restructure had streamlined some work but also left unanswered questions and new gaps. It was incredibly important. And once all that got ironed out, a lot of the conflict simply evaporated. And we know each other better. That's been huge to my learning about trust. I now think of trust not as something that necessarily comes first, but as something that kind of emerges after the fog clears. The fog masks what's important within and among us."

"Any broader, more systemic effects outside the team? How about all those stakeholders we talked about?"

"I'm not sure they noticed, as stakeholders only tend to squawk when things go wrong. But it's been really quiet on that front. That's a good sign. Here's one I didn't anticipate: The teams down below our leadership team members? Those 200 people? There are now quiet whispers about how we're more fun to watch. They experience less back-stabbing, fewer rumors, and more collaboration among us team members. I think we're confusing and demoralizing them less. By role modeling it, we're giving them implicit permission to work across functions. It's adding a depth and velocity to the organization I haven't seen before."

Orlando prods, "Have all of these changes shifted your own role?"

"Not hugely, but it gives me more time to focus on the things that are my primary responsibilities. Believe it or not, it now frees me up to leave here before 6 p.m. most days. And here's the irony. When we first met, I tested you two pretty hard about a Goodnight Moon value threshold. I think I asked the pointed question: is the time you two were going to suck up with this team building worth the hours team members would not get with their kids at night. I wanted to make sure we minimize the tax this put on them."

"Yeah, we remember," Orlando says with a smile.

"Well, the inverse appears true. I now have time to read that book to my 4-year old almost every night. You created a Goodnight Moon dividend with this work, at least in my house. It was an investment, not a tax, and the ROI is not only here, it's at bedtime. Tax versus investment. Those are two very different ways to see the resources of time and attention we put in.

Tom's eye's glisten a bit. "So...my wife and daughter thank you, too. And with that, I'll depart and let the three of you continue."

With Tom gone, Ava turns her attention to Juliette. "I can't put my finger on it, but something seems oddly different in your office. Did you change the lighting or something?"

"I was hoping you'd notice! It's the new fish tank. Come take a look," Juliette waves them over. "I think this one has more vibrancy. A calmer energy, more...ecosystem."

"This one has plants," observes Orlando.

"Two, to be exact. I got the new tank because I needed the plants."

"Nice, but I'm lost. Why the plants? Aesthetics?" asks Ava.

"No, I need a place to put you two. Ava, the first time we met, you asked me about whose fish tank it was. I mean, listen, I got it right away. I didn't know the answer, but I got your question. The tank is both mine and the fishes', right?"

"Yes." Huh. And I thought I was being so coy.

"Well, the two of you helped the team see that it's their tank, too. You've become part of our seascape, part of what shapes us and, I'd guess you've been shaped by us. I need you in the tank. It's part of your legacy."

"My goodness. I'm honored. That's a first. Where's Romeo 17?" asks Ava. "I don't see him."

"I came back from the trip to headquarters and found him floating belly-up."

"Aw, my condolences. So, is Romeo 18 in there yet?"

"No, no more Romeos. See that blue and yellow one? She's new. I was going to call her Jackie, as that's my wife's name. She's such a great leader in her own right. I asked her if I could use her name that way, but she was not honored by the gesture. So, I chose a different name."

"What's that?"

"Maya Gandalf, or MG for short. 'Maya' is for Maya Angelou. Her poem Phenomenal Woman (1978) has become a favorite of mine in the last few months. 'Now you understand Just why my head's not bowed.' Great poem. It helps me feel real and human in this corporate world. And 'Gandalf,' of course, is for one of the greatest leaders from all of literature (Tolkien, 1954). 'All we have to decide is what to do with the time that is given us,'" she imitates in her best Gandalf voice, miming the holding of a staff.

"I get all this now, better than I did. I'm both outside the team and inside it. It's a duality. From the outside, I have to make sure the tank has oxygen, light, and food, or the whole thing spirals downward. And from the inside, I'm one of them, in the ecosystem, a vital part of the we-ness of being in a tank. I get to—or have to—do a million things for this organization, but I discovered I'm the only one who gets to sit with and lead these people. That's a pretty cool honor, but it's also an immense responsibility. I've discovered that the more they own and engage, the better our lives are. I just have to figure out how to do that better and better.

"So, the answer to your question 'whose tank is it?' is: the tank belongs to the team members, or those who live inside it, and to the steward, she who cares for it. I just happen to be both."

"I think you and MG are going to be just fine," says Ava.

As they exit Juliette's office and turn toward the elevators, Orlando suggests a quick lunch. "There's a new fusion restaurant near the river. Eat and chat a bit? It would be great to debrief what we just heard from Juliette and Tom."

"I'd like that. I have to catch a flight later this afternoon, so a proper meal would be so nice."

SIXTEEN

A Wholesome Meal

Ava and Orlando ask for a table near the window. Midday sunlight streams through a glass vase filled with yellow and white tulips, striking a rich, vibrant contrast against the crisp, white tablecloth. A carafe of sparkling water silently bubbles.

"A toast to our team of two," smiles Ava.

"To us." The gleam in Orlando's eye speaks volumes.

"Orlando, I'm so curious. I know you were a bit apprehensive when we began this project. How has this played out for you? What have you discovered? For me, there have been so many moments on this project where I've deeply appreciated what you brought to our interactions. What's the story you're telling yourself about these months together?"

"Weird. Fun. Intense. I've felt new neurons connect, especially when I wasn't sure quite what was happening, or what particular experience we were trying to create for the team. But I liked it. It's the most I've learned in a long time. I can't say it's revolutionary for my practice, but it has opened my eyes and ears to entirely different ways of thinking about the work and what brings value, what clients need most, and how to partner. How about you?"

"Me too,' says Ava. "Over time, I've learned to enjoy these projects because the learning is so much edgier. Grittier. I've discovered I'm a bit of an addict for the adrenaline rush: the profound not-knowing of what their stories are, their context and complexity, their ongoing emergence. The dance. There's no good guy, no bad guy, just the darkness we get to help the team push away so they can make sense of whatever it is their light illumines for them. I'm always honored to help attend to that process."

"I like that. It's their darkness and their light. Who knows what they'll see when they look at things in new ways?"

"These fusion restaurant menus always make me scratch my head. What in the name of Julia Child are 'pork dumpling tostados? Anyway, what do you call this work, Ava? I think what we did was really good OD work, but literally, what do you call the thing we sold and delivered?"

"To be honest, I'm not sure. Sometimes I call it different things depending on how the client describes the problem they're facing."

"Do you call it 'Dialogic' something?"

"Dialogic OD? Maybe. While that's the theory base I most identify with and the mindset that infuses my work, our clients rarely know or care about our industry jargon or nomenclature. They just want to discover how their lives inside their team can be different tomorrow than they are today. A little less pain, a little more goodness.

"When they ask for training or team development, I often try to reframe this as helping them understand themselves better so that they can find their unique drivers for effectiveness. I think how effective they are together drives their internal experience and their external impact. I tend not to use the word 'performance' because it invariably leads to the conversation around 'how do we become a high performing team?' To that, I always say, 'Compared to whom or what? Why bother comparing?'"

Orlando extends the point. "It's not training, per se, but we do help them learn new knowledge and skills in real time. It's some process facilitation. I even heard you throw in some pop psychology."

"I agree," says Ava. "It's not facilitation, although that's a critical skill. It's a lot of narrative coaching, but not the in-depth stuff like you might do with an individual executive. It's coaching for the whole team together, including the leader."

Orlando nods. "We pulled from the best of both the Dialogic and Diagnostic mindsets and toolboxes. Maybe it's a huge Venn diagram of all these things. Whatever we call it, it's a creative process that demands in-the-moment courage."

Ava looks out the window. "Maybe you and I should just call this something for ourselves. Something that we'll write into the next contract we partner on. What's your recommendation?"

"I like 'Team Effectiveness Coaching' or 'Dialogic Team Effectiveness Coaching,'" says Orlando. "It just pulls it together. The focus is on the team, how we help them discover the dialogue they need to have, the effectiveness we help them unlock, and the coaching that gets them there."

"Sold."

They linger over coffee. Maybe neither quite wants this to end.

Orlando asks, "If they call us back to help again? Will it be easier?"

"In some ways, sure. If nothing else, we have a good baseline understanding of their world. But important things will have changed. They always do. We always do. If they invite us back, we'll need to start with a beginner's mind.

"That 'impromptu strategy meeting' Juliette went to? I heard through the grapevine that there's a possible acquisition in the works. Might buy a company or two while the industry consolidates. If that happens, it's likely Juliette will get promoted to SVP and have a larger org. I heard Craig wants to retire, and that Kelly might have to go on a leave of absence to handle some confidential medical things. But, as far as it went today, we've left them with a changed DNA and a set of capabilities they take forward individually and as a team, no matter where they go. And they all go somewhere.

"And I have to say it one more time. Thanks for saving me when I got so turned around during that one session. And for everything else. You've brought an incredible structured thinking and depth to our work together in ways big and small. I've learned a lot from you. There's no way I could have done this alone."

"You're welcome. I can only say the same to you. And I'm happy to partner with you anytime. It would be great to have you help out on one of my projects."

Reflection

Each time we enter the space of a team, it's as if the jigsaw puzzle inside the box has shifted. At one point, it tells a whole story, but not necessarily a logical or average or beautiful story, just a unique, wonderful, often absurd story, filled with discontinuities and paradoxes. Open the box again—with no picture on the cover—and now we see that familiar pieces have changed or left, and unfamiliar ones joined.

To be inside their box is to be part of an experience with its own logic, causality, and flow of discrete change events. To be outside their box and to enter it is to experience discontinuity. Our privilege is to be a bit player in their narrative for a brief moment.

Conclusion and Implications

Dialogic OD offers us a great frame or mindset for teams. It expands our painter's palette so that generative images can come to life. It equips us with the anthropologist's non-evaluative mindset. It lends us the evolutionary biologist's explanatory power of fit-for-use, adaptive theories of diversity within complexity.

From a process perspective, it helps bring the team itself *into* the things they can control. It eschews comparison, helping the team focus on themselves. It embraces data, especially the subjective data that the team creates and owns. The Dialogic lens broadens our views of what's possible. Infusing our work with both the Dialogic and the Diagnostic, we find immense strength and explanatory power. It amplifies our ability to focus on the good, true, and beautiful in teams.

Like our clients, we OD professionals swim in these very same seas of complexity and write our daily diaries of narrative. We are both in and of the systems we try to support. We try to stay true to a set of values passed down through generations. We put in our goggles the lenses of existing paradigms. We use our well-worn and beloved tool boxes.

But if our goggles have become fogged over time, if our worn tools don't solve contemporary issues like they once did, if our rigidness or inability to deal with complexity mirrors that of our clients, then it may help to discover some new manifestation of our practice. Available to us is the redirection of our energy toward mindsets that embrace our, and our client's, emergent, kaleidoscopic complexity and social construction of sense-making narratives. Redirection of that energy into experimentation with newer concepts involves taking risks that can have a potential payoff of greater long-term impact and relevance.

Perhaps this book in some small way fosters that ongoing dialogue. I'll add a few observations with the hope of continuing this dialogue in other forums.

As we become the un-experts in them and help *them* become the experts in themselves, the way we equip ourselves for this work shifts.

Subtly shifting the methods of our craft opens the door to bodies of skill and knowledge beyond the science of management and social psychology. Not unfamiliar perspectives and personas can add much to our endeavors, including our role as:

- curious anthropologists: watching, listening, asking;
- insightful counselors: eliciting deeper insights as awareness grows;
- courageous crucible holders: not afraid of the crackling of the refining fire;
- systemic ecologists: tending to systems of complex interaction;
- adaptive puzzle solvers: open to being surprised each time we open the box.

As we do this, certain questions lose relevance:

- How do we compare to other teams? *(We don't compare teams.)*
- Are we normal? *(We're most curious about what makes you unique.)*
- Do you get sick of working with abnormal teams like us? *(We don't think of you as abnormal, and we love our work with clients just like you.)*
- Is this model proven? *(The only model that needs to be proved is the one that helps you increase your effectiveness.)*
- Is the data valid? (*Because you create the data, it cannot be any more valid.)*

Reframing into a new set of questions helps the practitioner focus on being a great listener and a synthesizer, very attuned to the most important question that could be asked at this time. We free up our attention to key into their unspoken fear and aspiration. We can be supportive, empathic, systemic, curious, pragmatic, validating, and explorative without analyzing, comparing, assessing, or fixing.

In sum, while the Dialogic mindset offers practitioners the wonderful gift of liberation from previous mental models that limit how we see teams, it simultaneously confers to us the responsibility—or challenge—

to reimagine our work for the good of the client. Rather than thinking about organizations as "objects to be scientifically investigated, ensuring conversations convey objective reality (just the facts), and change as something that is episodic and can be planned and managed," (Marshak, 2020) we may instead take up the challenge to embrace ambiguity, uncertainty, and nonlinearity even more foundationally—even when doing so makes us feel awkward or vulnerable. It asks us to help our client teams find coherence and logic on their own terms, not on ours. It asks us to be consciously aware of and frame our own use of power, models, methodologies, and tools in pursuit of the client's ownership of the current and future state. It asks us to enter the client's flowing "river of existence," be it upstream in rushing mountain streams or in quiet, deep, deltas, respecting the past, present, and future as a continuum, knowing that we will soon exit that river.

This hard work is ours: to co-create with them elegant frames for inquiry and action. In this liminal moment for OD, our tool boxes can be filled with a rich mix of both Dialogic and Diagnostic methods that in the hands of wise and capable practitioners help our clients adapt and thrive in a complex world.

Totally doable.

References

Angelou, Maya. (1978). *Phenomenal Woman: Four Poems Celebrating Women.* New York, NY: Random House.

Block, P. (2018). *Community: The Structure of Belonging.* Oakland, CA: Berrett-Koehler.

Box, George E. P. (1976). Science and Statistics. *Journal of the American Statistical Association*, 71:356, 791–799. doi:10.1080/01621459.1976.10480949

Bushe, G.R. (2020). *The Dynamics of Generative Change.* North Vancouver, BC: BMI.

Bushe, G.R. & R.J. Marshak (eds.)(2015). *Dialogic Organization Development: The Theory and Practice of Transformational Change.* Oakland, CA: Berrett-Koehler.

Bushe, G.R. & Marshak, R.J. (2009). Revisioning Organization Development. Diagnostic and Dialogic Premises and Patterns of Practice. *Journal of Applied Behavioral Science,* 45:3, 348-368.

DeGeneres, Ellen. (2001). Ellen DeGeneres Sits Down with *The Four Agreements* Author don Miguel Ruiz. *O, The Oprah Magazine.* Retrieved from www.oprah.com

Didion, Joan. (2006). *We Tell Ourselves Stories in Order to Live: Collected Nonfiction.* New York, NY: Alfred A. Knopf.

Emanuel, S., Kennedy, K., Shearmur, A., & Edwards, G. (2016). *Rogue One: A Star Wars Story.* USA: Walt Disney Studio Motion Pictures.

Eoyang, G. H., & Holladay, R. J. (2013). *Adaptive Action: Leveraging Uncertainty in Your Organization.* Stanford, CA: Stanford University Press.

Firth, D. (2020). *Unconditional Communication: Shaping Better Relationships and Bigger Futures—Together.* Colorado, USA: Lagado Library Publications.

Fuller, R. B. (1964, November 3). *Christian Science Monitor.*

Homer-Dixon, Thomas. (2009). The Newest Science: Replacing Physics, Ecology Will Be the Master Science of the 21st Century. *Alternatives Journal*, 4, 8–38.

Kazantzakis, Nikos. (1952). *Zorba the Greek.* New York, NY: Simon & Schuster.

King, G., Rosen, O., & Tanner, M. (2004). Information in Ecological Inference: An Introduction. In G. King, O. Rosen, & M. Tanner (Eds.), Ecological Inference: New Methodological Strategies (Analytical Methods for Social Research, pp. 1-12). Cambridge: Cambridge University Press.

Lewis, C. S. (1955). *The Magician's Nephew.* London: The Bodley Head.

Lipmanowicz, H., & McCandless, K. (2014). *The Surprising Power of Liberating Structures: Simple Rules to Unleash a Culture of Innovation.* Liberating Structures Press.

Lucas, G. (1999). *Star Wars, Episode I: The Phantom Menace.* USA: Twentieth Century Fox.

Marshak, R. J. (2020). *Dialogic Process Consulting: Generative Meaning Making in Action.* North Vancouver, BC: BMI Publishing.

Miller, Henry. (1957). *Big Sur and the Oranges of Hieronymus Bosch.* New York, NY: New Directions Publishing.

Quinn, Robert. E. (2004). *Building the Bridge as You Walk on It: A Guide for Leading Change.* San Francisco, CA: Jossey-Bass.

Rodgers, C. (2013). *Taking Organizational Complexity Seriously.* London, UK: Center for Progressive Leadership.

Rose, T. (2016). *The End of Average: Unlocking Our Potential by Embracing What Makes Us Different.* New York, NY: HarperCollins Publishers.

Substance Abuse and Mental Health Services Administration. (2019). Key substance use and mental health indicators in the United States: Results from the 2018 National Survey on Drug Use and Health (HHS Publication No. PEP19-5068, NSDUH Series H-54). Rockville, MD: Center for Behavioral Health Statistics and Quality, Substance Abuse and Mental Health Services Administration. Retrieved from https://www.samhsa.gov/data

Tolkien, J. R. R. (1954). *The Fellowship of the Ring.* London: George Allen & Unwin.

BMI Series in Dialogic OD

The BMI series in Dialogic OD, inspired by the original Addison-Wesley Series in OD, is a series of short, 100 page volumes written by experienced Dialogic OD practitioners. Edited by Gervase Bushe and Bob Marshak, each narrowly focuses on one specific aspect of Dialogic OD practice and provides consultants with tested, practical models and processes, along with case examples to make the models come alive.

Dialogic Process Consulting: Generative Meaning-Making in Action

https://b-m-institute.com/books/dialogic-process-consulting/

Robert Marshak introduces a subtle but powerful dialogic OD method that coaches and consultants can use to help clients address limiting assumptions and create new possibilities. The phrase "generative meaning-making in action" captures the essence of the approach. You will learn how to identify and address out-of-awareness mindsets during everyday conversations, how to deeply listen for the implicit mindsets that influence meaning-making in individuals, groups and organizations, and how to intervene through transforming talk to challenge or change them.

The Dynamics of Generative Change

https://b-m-institute.com/books/the-dynamics-of-generative-change/

Gervase Bushe steps you through the Generative Change Model, a way to approach organizational change more aligned with today's needs for an agile and engaged workforce than planned change methods. We follow the case of Consolidated Construction Materials Supply, 200 poorly engaged employees inside a large, traditional construction company. Organized into three fragmented units, this low-tech warehouse and distribution operation transformed into a highly engaged, collaborative, agile and fully digitized one in a little more than two years after the first phone call between the consultant and the Director. They accomplished this without a vision, without a plan, without training, any resistance to change, and only 1 external OD consultant. The book provides advice on the key issues in leading an emergent, generative change process.

Hosting Generative Change: Creating Containers for Creativity and Commitment

http://b-m-institute.com/books/hosting-generative-change/

When the future is uncertain and the past is contested, good hosting can bring hope and co-operation into the present. Any Dialogic OD practice will bring people together for creative conversations, expanded horizons, mutual connection and committed action. The way these events are hosted can make all the difference. **Mark McKergow** brings over a decade of research into the etiquette of hosting in different cultures and eras and combines it with three decades of practice in organizational development and change. The book offers an image of superb hosting as a mix of detailed planning and openness to whatever emerges, taking the lead when needed, with the intent of stepping back as quickly as possible so participants can lead themselves. The book offers a framework of six hosting roles to help navigate the inevitable ups and downs of working with large (and small) groups.

The Team Discovered: Dialogic Team Coaching

http://b-m-institute.com/books/the-team-discovered/

This hopeful, poignant, and deeply insightful book brings the wisdom of Dialogic OD and the heritage of Diagnostic OD into an expansive view of how to best support teams in a world of immense diversity and attention poverty. **Bennett Bratt** offers a new approach to team development that meets today's teams where they live: in a complex world with intense demands and precious little time. This book challenges widely used approaches to team development that utilize data showing a gap between current and desirable team performance. Most methods presume some kind of evaluative comparison is helpful: comparison to other groups, comparison to large data sets, comparison to best practices, comparison to a theoretical ideal. Instead, Ben explains why a dialogic approach to the use of questionnaire data is better at helping teams author their own narrative of effectiveness, one they will own and live into. While showing how to make data useful, Bratt persuasively argues that comparison is at best, a distraction and at worst, debilitating. The book illustrates how to bring the mindsets and tools of Dialogic OD to team coaching through an extended case example.

Future Planned Volumes

Making Every Conversation Generative

Jackie Stavros & Cheri Torres

Entry and Contracting for Dialogic OD

Tova Averbuch

It's a Thing: Using Transactional Objects in Dialogic OD

Tonnie van der Zouwen

If you have an idea for a short (under 30,000 words) book on a specific aspect of Dialogic OD practice, please contact either Gervase (**bushe@sfu.ca**) or Bob (**bobmarshak@aol.com**) to discuss.

Made in the USA
Monee, IL
17 May 2022